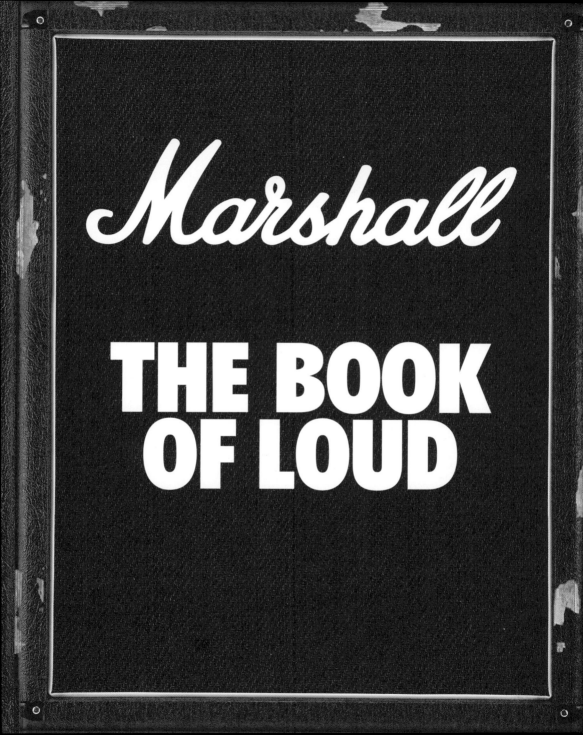

Marshall

THE BOOK OF LOUD

THE BOOK OF LOUD

AN ESSENTIAL MISCELLANY OF MUSICAL KNOWLEDGE

NICK HARPER

MITCHELL BEAZLEY

An Hachette UK Company
www.hachette.co.uk

First published in Great Britain in 2016
by Mitchell Beazley, a division of
Octopus Publishing Group Ltd
Carmelite House
50 Victoria Embankment
London EC4Y 0DZ

www.octopusbooks.co.uk
www.octopusbooksusa.com

Copyright © Octopus Publishing Group Limited 2016

Distributed in the US by
Hachette Book Group
1290 Avenue of the Americas
4th and 5th Floors
New York, NY 10020

Distributed in Canada by
Canadian Manda Group
664 Annette St.
Toronto, Ontario, Canada M6S 2C8

Nick Harper has asserted his right under the Copyright,
Designs and Patents Act 1988 to be identified as
the author of this work.

ISBN 978 1 78472 225 8

A CIP catalogue record for this book is available from
the British Library.

Printed and bound in China.

10 9 8 7 6 5 4 3 2 1

Commissioning Editor Joe Cottington
Illustrators Grace Helmer, Ben Tallon,
  and Amber Badger
Senior Editor Pauline Bache
Designer Geoff Fennell
Art Director Juliette Norsworthy
Picture Library Manager Jennifer Veall
Senior Production Manager Katherine Hockley

CONTENTS

★·★·★·★·★·★·★·★·★·★·★·★·★·★·★·★·☆·★·★·★·★·★·★·★·★·★·★·★·★·★·★·★·★·★

NO MATTER WHO YOU ARE,
NO MATTER WHERE YOU ARE FROM,
OR WHAT YOUR BACKGROUND IS,
ONE THING CAN UNITE US ALL – MUSIC.

IT'S SELF-EXPRESSION.
IT'S FEELING THE CONNECTION. IT'S LAUGHING.
IT'S CRYING. IT'S INSPIRING. IT'S CONCERTS.
IT'S FESTIVALS.
IT'S THE TIME OF YOUR LIFE.

MUSIC IS MAGICAL.
WE LOVE EVERYTHING ABOUT IT
– THE PEOPLE, THE SCENE, THE LIFESTYLE.
WE LIVE FOR MUSIC.

INTRODUCTION

THE YEAR 1955 IS, ACCORDING TO LEGEND, THE YEAR THAT ROCK MUSIC WAS CREATED. THAT WAS THE YEAR SCHMALTZ AND THE BLUES COLLIDED TO FORM A GENRE OF MUSIC WITH AN ALTOGETHER HARDER EDGE. THAT WAS THE YEAR ROCK MUSIC WAS TRULY BORN.

Yet we at Marshall believe rock was born much earlier than that. On 29 July 1923, to be exact, in the west London suburb of Kensington. That was the day James Charles Marshall was born.

Jim Marshall grew up to be the man who invented the most iconic amplifier on the planet: the Marshall amp. In doing so, the "Father of Loud" changed the landscape of rock music forever.

Without Jim Marshall and the Marshall amp, Pete Townshend may never have found the sound or volume he was desperately looking for. Without the Marshall amp, Jimi Hendrix's psychedelic assault may never have sounded like such a seismic shift from all that had gone before. And without Marshall's influence on so many of the rock legends who strode through the 1960s and 70s, we may never have heard the later generations they inspired to pick up a guitar and make their own noise.

Jim Marshall is no longer with us but his drive and ambition live on in everything we build and everything we do. Every Marshall amp, every cabinet, pedal and headphone we create is built to make everything sound better, and not just "one louder" better – although we've done that too.

Over the last 50 years Marshall amps have been used by some of the biggest bands and rock stars of all time, from AC/DC to Aerosmith,

The Who to Paul Weller, from Blur to Muse and on and on. The Marshall black box has gained legendary status among rock's greatest names.

And the very best choose Marshall because they recognize that we are driven by the same thing that drives them: a lifelong passion for rock. We love everything about this music. Everything about the scene, the people, the lifestyle. We live for everything rock music represents. And given that you are reading this book, we're guessing that you do too. Which brings us to where we are right now.

Welcome to *The Book Of Loud*, a book that sums up our love of and commitment to rock music. What you have in your hands is an unashamed celebration of rock in all its many magnificent forms, an ode to music's greatest genre.

In these pages we lift the lid on everything that matters in rock music. From the world's greatest guitarists and rock's greatest riffs through to the loudest acts on the planet and the correct etiquette for stage diving. We cover the feuds and the festivals, the records and the riders, the legends and the lunacy. Put simply, every rock nugget worth knowing.

So, turn it up to 11 and turn the page. And for those about to rock, we salute you.

THE MARSHALL STORY

A HISTORY OF **LOUD!**

FEW MEN HAVE HELPED TO SHAPE THE HISTORY OF ROCK MUSIC TO THE SAME DEGREE AS JIM MARSHALL. FOR MORE THAN HALF A CENTURY, HIS ICONIC MARSHALL AMP HAS HELPED PUSH ROCK MUSIC TO NEW HEIGHTS. THIS IS THE GREAT MAN'S STORY.

1923

James Charles Marshall is born in Kensington, London, England, on 29 July. As a young man with no formal education, "Jim" tries out a number of jobs before taking up drumming professionally in the 1940s.

1953

Jim opens his own drumming school. His students include Mitch Mitchell (The Jimi Hendrix Experience) and Micky Waller (Little Richard), among many others. From the profits of teaching around 65 drummers a week, he saves the money to open a second, more lucrative business.

JULY 1962

Jim opens a music shop with his son, Terry, called J & T Marshall at 76 Uxbridge Road in Hanwell, west London, selling all manner of musical instruments, from woodwind and brass to Jim's favourite: drums. When a regular customer, a guitarist called Pete Townshend, complains that he can't make the noises he'd like to make, Jim and his team set about producing an amplifier that will make this possible.

SEPTEMBER 1962

After a number of prototypes, the very first Marshall amplifier is born, affectionately named "Number One". It is the forerunner of the legendary JTM45 amp, named after

Jim and his son, Terry. Placed in the window of Jim's shop, 23 orders are taken on the very first day, including one from Pete Townshend, soon-to-be lead guitarist of The Who.

1965

Again at the request of Townshend, and after much trial and error, Jim stacks four 12in speakers together in a cabinet in the quest for more power – and in doing so, creates the basis for the legendary "Marshall stack". As portable as it was powerful, the stack would soon dominate the sound of rock 'n' roll, across the world and through the decades.

1966-80

As the company's reputation and legend grow, over the next two decades the greatest guitarists on earth seek out Marshall cabinets – from Jimi Hendrix (middle name, fittingly: Marshall) and Jimmy Page to Eric Clapton and Angus Young. The original design remains largely untouched until 1981.

1981

The groundbreaking JCM 800 series is introduced, boasting a more aggressive, modern sound. It takes its name from Jim Marshall's initials (his middle name is Charles).

1981-2012

As the decades pass, Marshall adds a number of new models to its catalogue – including the all-valve JVM Series in 2007 and the Class 5 in

2011. As the decades pass, the company adds a whole new generation of guitar disciples to its ranks, including Guns N' Roses' Slash, Jane's Addiction's Dave Navarro, and Slipknot's Corey Taylor, to name just a few. Along the way, in 2003, Jim Marshall is appointed an OBE (Officer of the Most Excellent Order of the British Empire) for his services to music and charity.

2012

On 5 April 2012, Jim Marshall, "the Father of Loud" passes away, aged 88. "Rock 'n' roll will never be the same without him," tweets Slash. Mötley Crüe's Nikki Sixx is another of many paying tribute, adding that Marshall was "responsible for some of the greatest audio moments in music's history – and 50 per cent responsible for all our hearing loss".

2016

Today, the company Jim built continues to refine its amps and redefine rock music as we hear it, having added headphones and speakers to its range in recent years. Clearly, while Jim Marshall may no longer be with us, his Legacy of Loud rocks on and on.

THE ART OF NOISE

Several bands that have routinely turned their volumes
up to 11 and beyond.

10dB	**Breathing** (barely audible).
50dB	**Conversation at home.**
85dB	**The point at which noise is considered dangerous.** Anything over this can potentially cause permanent hearing loss or damage.
100dB	**Jet take-off or overhead at 305m (1,000ft).**
108–114dB	**Most live rock music.**
117dB	**DEEP PURPLE** Having reached 117dB at London's Rainbow Theatre in 1972, powered by their 10,000-watt Marshall PA system, Deep Purple's sonic assault in an intimate, 3,000-seat venue left three fans unconscious but earned them the accolade of the world's loudest band.
126dB	**THE WHO** Having registered a Guinness World Record in hitting 126dB during a gig in 1976, The Who's Pete Townshend helped establish Hearing Education and Awareness for Rockers (H.E.A.R.), an organization created by veteran rock stars who exposed themselves to damaging levels of noise. Townshend himself suffers from tinnitus, a permanent ringing in his ears.

129.5dB	**MANOWAR**
	New York noise-mongers Manowar registered 129.5dB in 1984, earning themselves a Guinness World Record for loudest musical performance. Realizing the ill effects extreme noise can have on listeners' ears, Guinness stopped recognizing this particular record soon after.
130dB	**AC/DC**
	During 1980–81's "Back in Black" tour, the legendarily loud Aussie rockers hit 130dB. They could have gone at least one point louder, had the promoter not requested they turn it down.
130dB	**LED ZEPPELIN**
	Already suspected to be pushing the boundaries of loud, confirmation arrived in 1969 when the American Speech-Language-Hearing Association recorded Led Zep's performance of *Heartbreaker* at 130dB.
130dB	**MOTÖRHEAD**
	For a band whose artistic output included the long-player *Everything Louder than Everyone Else*, noise came as standard. Lemmy and Co. routinely hit between 120 and 123dB and were reported to have reached 130dB at a 1984 performance, causing the plaster on the ceiling of the Cleveland Variety Theater to crumble and fall.
132.5dB	**GALLOWS**
	Eyeing up Manowar's record, British punk band Gallows claimed to have gone all the way up to an ear-shredding 132.5dB.
136dB	**KISS**
	Arguably ridiculous, undeniably loud. In 2009, the glam metallers hit 136dB in a performance in Ottawa, Canada. They were forced to turn it down after the police responded to neighbours' not-unreasonable complaints.
150dB	**Jet take-off at 25m (82ft).** Extended exposure to this can lead to eardrum rupture.

ROCK RIDERS

❖❖❖ ❖❖❖ ❖❖❖ ❖❖❖ ❖❖❖ ❖❖❖ ❖❖❖ ❖❖❖ ❖❖❖ ❖❖❖ ❖❖❖ ❖❖❖

What musicians request when they're on the road.

JOHNNY CASH

On tour in 1993, The Man in Black had himself a raging thirst. His request included: *"Coffee – one gallon, milk, sugar, etc. Coca-Cola Classic – one dozen. Spring drinking water – a half-gallon. Please – no substitutions of soft-drink brands."* It probably wasn't all for him. And feeling patriotic, the former US bomb-disposal operative also requested *"an American Flag on a pole stand (typical size 3' by 5')"*, to be placed *"on stage in full view of the audience throughout the show"*.

RED HOT CHILI PEPPERS

In 2000, the ageing rockers (still) requested *"six pairs of white crew socks"*, suggesting old habits die hard. To this they added: *"One pair of plaid cotton boxer shorts; two aromatherapy-type candles; 24 one-liter. bottles of still 'glacier' water (served at room temperature); small bowls of whole, pitted dates, figs and raw, unsalted cashews; and a Meditation Room (small in size)."* Rock 'n' roll.

FOO FIGHTERS

A 2008 rider for Dave Grohl and Co. kept things amusingly simple, asking for *"Eight beers (Coors Light/cans), four bottles of Gatorade (Remember: wacky colours, please), two toothbrushes and two small hand sanitizers"*. It also noted that *"any effort to make the dressing room comfy and sexy is much appreciated. We like to lounge about and convalesce in the dressing room. So feel free to shoplift some cool Ikea furniture."*

IGGY AND THE STOOGES

On tour in 2006, Iggy – or one of his people – penned a now legendary rider that was long and had its tongue firmly in its cheek. Abridged here, it requested *"Two bottles of smooth, full-bodied, Bordeaux-type red wine. Probably French. And something we've heard of and still can't pronounce. Look, there's f*cking loads of good red wines. Ask the man in the wine shop"*. Plus *"One case of big bottles of good, premium beer. Here's a clue – it probably won't start with a letter 'B' and end with 'udweiser'. One case of cans of assorted sodas. Ginger beer? Dandelion and burdock? I don't know. Lemonade? Lots and lots of clean ice. Not ice that a polar bear has been standing on, with its big mucky feet. Cauliflower/ broccoli, cut into individual florets and thrown immediately into the garbage. I f*cking hate that."*

AC/DC

By 2008, the hard-rocking Aussie legends were perhaps beginning to feel their age. Their rider requested a *"small selection of imported cheeses and crackers (English cheeses and water crackers preferred), one box of Twinings English Breakfast Tea, 50 packets of sugar"*. In a nod to excess, there was booze, but not much, just *"one case of bottled Heineken"*. And, most tellingly of all, they also specified that *"three oxygen tanks with three masks must be at the venue at load-in"*.

Source: www.thesmokinggun.com

TOP OF THE POPS

A recap of all 17 of The Beatles' UK number ones.

TITLE	★	WEEK ENDING	WEEKS AT NUMBER ONE
From Me to You	★	2 May 1963	7
She Loves You	★	12 September 1963	6
I Want to Hold Your Hand	★	2 December 1963	5
Can't Buy Me Love	★	2 April 1964	3
A Hard Day's Night	★	23 July 1964	3
I Feel Fine	★	10 December 1964	5
Ticket to Ride	★	22 April 1965	3
Help!	★	5 August 1965	3
Day Tripper/We Can Work It Out	★	16 December 1965	5
Paperback Writer	★	23 June 1966	2
Eleanor Rigby/Yellow Submarine	★	18 August 1966	4
All You Need Is Love	★	19 July 1967	3
Hello, Goodbye	★	6 December 1967	7
Lady Madonna	★	27 March 1968	2
Hey Jude	★	11 September 1968	2
Get Back	★	23 April 1969	6
Ballad of John and Yoko	★	11 June 1969	3

NOTE: The Beatles' run of 11 consecutive number ones came to an end in February 1967, when *Strawberry Fields Forever* was beaten to top spot by Engelbert Humperdinck's *Release Me*.

ROCK ★ KNOWLEDGE

One of rock's most enduring conspiracy theories has it that The Beatles' Paul McCartney actually died in a car crash in 1966 and was replaced by a lookalike. Fuelling the speculation, the band's *Revolution 9* contains a section which, when played backward, says: "Turn me on, dead man". In *Strawberry Fields Forever*, John Lennon added further fuel by saying: "I buried Paul", until he later explained he actually said "cranberry sauce". Despite the claims, all evidence suggests Macca is alive, well, and hoisting two thumbs up.

"HAND ME THAT GLOCKENSPIEL!"

Unexpected percussion instruments in rock.

GLOCKENSPIEL

A series of graduated metal bars tuned to the chromatic scale, played with two hammers.

Hear it on: *No Surprises* by Radiohead

MARACAS

Two long-handled, hollow-topped percussion instruments, the heads filled with beads or beans and shaken to make noise.

Hear it on: *You Can't Always Get What You Want* by The Rolling Stones

HARPSICHORD

Similar to a piano but with strings plucked rather than struck.

Hear it on: *Too Afraid to Love You* by The Black Keys

MELODICA

Aka a wind piano, this is blown like a horn and played like a piano.

Hear it on: *Champagne Supernova* by Oasis

BAGPIPES

A big bag full of air, the noise here is created as the air is squeezed out.

Hear it on: *It's a Long Way to the Top (If You Wanna Rock 'n' Roll)* by AC/DC

HURDY-GURDY

Stringed instrument played by turning a handle.

Hear it on: *Gallows Pole* by Led Zeppelin

ONDES MARTENOT

An electronic instrument invented in 1928, now played either via a keyboard or metal ring with the right hand while the left controls the volume, timbre and percussive attack of each note with a control panel.

Hear it on: *Idioteque* by Radiohead

KAZOO

Mouth instrument consisting of small metal or plastic tube with a side hole covered by a thin membrane – gives the human voice a buzzing quality.

Hear it on: *Crosstown Traffic* by Jimi Hendrix (although he used a comb and some cellophane)

MARIMBA

A wooden-keyed xylophone.

Hear it on: *The Nurse* by The White Stripes

SPOONS

Just spoons.

Hear it on: *Spoonman* by Soundgarden

SIZE MATTERS

✶ ✶

The journey from vinyl to MP3.

1894
78rpm record

Launched by Berliner Gramophone, the first US flat-disc record label, 78s were constructed of a shellac compound. Double-sided records appeared in 1907.

1948
33¹/₃ rpm LP

Launched by Columbia Records, initially running 17 minutes per side.

1949
45rpm record

A replacement for the 78, launched by RCA-Victor.

1963
Cassette

Launched by Philips as the Compact Cassette. The cassette-playing Walkman arrived in 1979.

1965
8-track cartridge

Launched by Ford Motor Company, assisted by RCA-Victor, as early in-car entertainment.

1982
Compact Disc

Launched by Sony and Philips.

1992
MiniDisc

Launched by Sony.

1998
MP3 player

Launched by South Korean company SaeHan Information Systems (MPMan F10). The iPod arrived in 2001.

FROM AB/CD TO ZED LEP

A princely selection of rock doppelgängers
and tribute acts.

ROCK	MOCK
AC/DC	AB/CD
Arctic Monkeys	Antarctic Monkeys
Black Sabbath	Blackest Sabbath
Bon Jovi	Non Jovi
Fleetwood Mac	Fleetwood Mock
Foo Fighters	Four Fighters
Iron Maiden	Hi-on Maiden
Kings of Leon	Kins of Leon
Meat Loaf	Maet Loaf
Metallica	Misstallica
Oasis	Oasish
Ozzy Osbourne	Ozzy OzzSpawn
Nirvana	Nearvana
Motörhead	Motörheadache
The Killers	The Fillers
The Rolling Stones	The Rollin' Clones
R.E.M.	aRe wE theM
The Beatles	The Dung Beatles
The Doors	The Back Doors
U2	U2-2
Yes	No
Led Zeppelin	Zed Leppelin

HELLO CLEVELAND!

Rock's longest, seemingly never-ending
world tour…

On 11 November 2009, New York three-piece Thirty Seconds to Mars played a live date at La Cigalle in Paris, France, the first of a string of dates that would take in Cologne, Milan, Amsterdam, London, and Berlin before seeing them head back to perform on home soil. So far, so expected for a touring rock band with a new album to air.

Unlike other tours by other bands, however, this one just didn't end. By June 2010, the group had racked up 100 gigs, which soon became 200 by February 2011, then began its slow but inevitable climb toward 300.

Finally, as fatigue set in, Thirty Seconds to Mars set the final date on their never-ending tour. On 7 December 2011, more than two years after they first set out, the tour ended at New York's Hammerstein Ballroom, where the 309th gig set a new world record. "It was the journey of a lifetime," wheezed frontman Jared Leto.

NOTABLE ROCK-STAR TATTOOS

Nowadays every self-respecting rock star has ink. But some tats are more notable than others.

NAME	BAND	BODY PART	TATTOO design/wording
Pete Doherty/ Carl Barât	The Libertines	Left forearm/right bicep	"Libertine"
Frank Carter	Gallows	Chest	Double-eagle crest
Travis Barker	Blink-182	Stomach	**Boombox** (inspired by his childhood love of breakdancing)
Simon Neil	Biffy Clyro	Chest	"God Only Knows What I'd Be Without You"
Alex Turner	Arctic Monkeys	Left forearm	**Yorkshire Rose** (Turner was born in Sheffield, Yorkshire, England)
Henry Rollins	Black Flag	Back	"Search And Destroy"
Beth Ditto	Gossip	Left shoulder	"Mama" anchor
Billie Joe Armstrong	Green Day	Right forearm	Filmstrip of his wife, Adrienne
Brad Nowell	Sublime	Right forearm	"Sublime" (as seen on the cover of the band's debut album)
Nathan & Caleb Followill	Kings of Leon	Right and left shoulder respectively	Grizzly bear paw
Josh Homme	Queens of the Stone Age	Knuckles	"Cam"/"Cap"
Anthony Kiedis	Red Hot Chili Peppers	Back	A massive Haida Thunderbird
Björk	Björk	Upper left arm	**Viking compass** ("So I don't get lost.")
Tommy Lee	Mötley Crüe	Stomach	"Mayhem"
Pete Wentz	Fall Out Boy	Right arm	**Jack Skellington** (character in Tim Burton's *The Nightmare Before Christmas*)
Marilyn Manson	Marilyn Manson	Right arm	**Green cyclops** (based on a drawing Manson did)

ARE YOU SITTING COMFORTABLY?

For some bands and artists, a classic track cannot be rushed.
Rock history is littered with tracks that didn't want to end.

9 minutes, 59 seconds
I'm Your Captain by Grand Funk Railroad

10 minutes, 21 seconds
Maggot Brain by Funkadelic

10 minutes, 30 seconds
Achilles' Last Stand by Led Zeppelin

10 minutes, 45 seconds
Marquee Moon by Television

11 minutes, 08 seconds
In My Time of Dying by Led Zeppelin

11 minutes, 19 seconds
Desolation Row by Bob Dylan

11 minutes, 34 seconds
The End by The Doors

11 minutes, 37 seconds
The Low Spark of High-heeled Boys by Traffic

12 minutes, 24 seconds
Starless by King Crimson

14 minutes, 59 seconds
Voodoo Chile by The Jimi Hendrix Experience

16 minutes, 14 seconds
Salisbury by Uriah Heep

17 minutes, 04 seconds
In-A-Gadda-Da-Vida by Iron Butterfly

17 minutes, 31 seconds
Sister Ray by The Velvet Underground

17 minutes, 31 seconds

In Held 'Twas in I by Procul Harum

20 minutes, 32 seconds

2112 by Rush

21 minutes, 49 seconds

The Gates of Delirium by Yes

23 minutes, 03 seconds

Supper's Ready by Genesis

23 minutes, 32 seconds

Echoes by Pink Floyd

23 minutes, 58 seconds

Octavarium by Dream Theater

30 minutes, 25 seconds

The Ikon by Todd Rundgren's Utopia

43 minutes, 50 seconds

Thick as a Brick by Jethro Tull

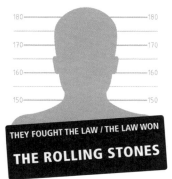

THEY FOUGHT THE LAW / THE LAW WON

THE ROLLING STONES

In a career as long as the Stones have enjoyed, you might expect their number to have fallen foul of the law on occasion. Mick Jagger, Brian Jones, and Bill Wyman's most notable run-in was of an unexpected nature, occurring in 1965 on the way home from a gig. Desperate to answer the call of nature, the three Stones rolled into a service station in London's East Ham and asked to use the facilities. When denied the key by the station attendant, Jagger announced: "We'll piss anywhere, man" – the service station wall being the particular target. The police arrived almost immediately and the three were nabbed, charged, and fined five pounds apiece.

ANATOMY OF... **A DRUMKIT**

To play the drums, you must first understand the drums.

TOM-TOMS

Usually comprised of a floor, mid and high tom, tom-toms essentially add depth to the sound. The high produces a higher pitch than the mid and floor toms. Some drummers replace the mid tom-tom with a ride cymbal.

SNARE DRUM AND BASS DRUM

Complementing components, the bass produces the low, boomy sound, driving the rhythm and keeping everything in time. Beads on the bottom of the snare drum produce their trademark "snare-y" sound.

CYMBALS

Hi-hat, ride and crash ride cymbals are present on most sets. The hi-hat is the most controllable, altering the sound by opening or closing it; the ride often acts as a second hi-hat. The crash is a nice addition, literally producing a crashing noise.

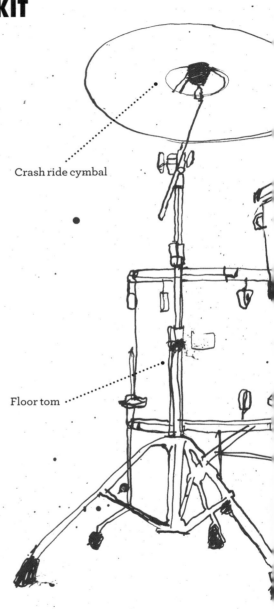

Crash ride cymbal

Floor tom

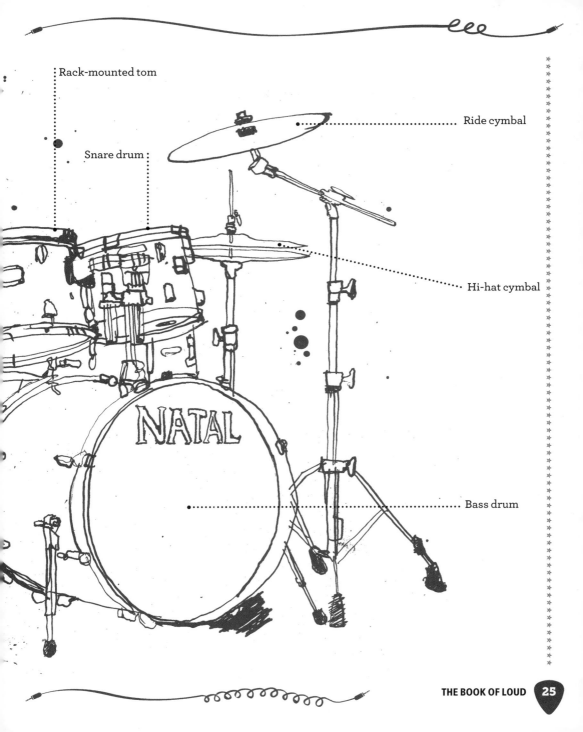

Rack-mounted tom

Snare drum

Ride cymbal

Hi-hat cymbal

Bass drum

NATAL

I'M WITH THE BANNED

In 2001, Clear Channel Communications – the largest owner of radio stations across the USA – issued a very, very long list of songs its stations might avoid playing in the weeks following the attack on New York's Twin Towers. The list ranged from understandable to nonsensical and included the following…

Jump
by Van Halen

Stairway to Heaven
by Led Zeppelin

Aeroplane
by Red Hot Chili Peppers

Ticket to Ride
by The Beatles

Knockin' on Heaven's Door
by Bob Dylan

Benny and the Jets
by Elton John

Brain Stew
by Green Day

Great Balls of Fire
by Jerry Lee Lewis

Ruby Tuesday
by The Rolling Stones

Free Fallin'
by Tom Petty

I'm Goin' Down
by Bruce Springsteen

In the Air Tonight
by Phil Collins

We Gotta Get Out of This Place
by The Animals

ROCK KNOWLEDGE

In 1985, Marshall amps founder Jim Marshall had his hand prints added to Hollywood's Rock and Roll Walk of Fame. "As I was putting my hand prints in [to the cement]," said Jim, "I thought, 'Good God! I've really arrived!"

AMPS AND INK

Rock music and tattoos go together like tequila and salt, Rolls-Royces and swimming pools. We asked five of the UK's hottest tattooists to give our JMV Series an added rock 'n' roll look for our Marshall Design Store. Here are some of the results…

ANTONY FLEMMING

EMILY WOOD

ROCK KNOWLEDGE

The London Calling of the classic Clash track came from a BBC catchphrase during World War II: "Good morning, America," it announced. "This is London calling."

PHIL KYLE

TUTTI SERRA

VICKY MORGAN

In this series, we have chosen some of our favourite performers; the artists who embody the Marshall spirit. These are some of the true pioneers of rock – the Legends of Loud.

LEMMY
The Ace of Spades

He lived fast, but somehow, despite his best efforts, Lemmy just wouldn't die young.

He was born Ian Kilmister in Stoke-on-Trent, England on Christmas Eve 1945. The nickname was said to have come from his love of slot machines – "Lemme have a quid [pound]!" The name soon stuck and the legend quickly grew.

Via a stint in a washing-machine factory, Lemmy served his rock apprenticeship as a roadie for Jimi Hendrix, but having witnessed Hendrix's guitar heroics, he switched from lead guitar to bass and joined Hawkwind before forming his own band in 1975. He wanted to call his group "Bastard", but his manager persuaded him "Motörhead" might stand a better chance. Twenty-two studio albums followed over the next four decades, including the signature *Ace of Spades* – "It's not a song; it's the ultimate monster," he later explained. During that time band members came and went, but Lemmy remained the one true constant and grew to be an icon of rock.

His distorted bass anchored a rawness and brutality never bettered by Motörhead's peers. He described it as classic rock 'n 'roll, not heavy metal, but members of Metallica were just some of the many young admirers who begged to differ.

When he died, in late 2015, cancer took the credit. Lemmy reached 70, despite smoking like a chimney and imbibing a bottle of Jack Daniel's every day, though in later years he replaced that with vodka on doctor's orders. "I've had a whale of a time out of rock 'n' roll," he said before the end, "and rock 'n' roll has had a whale of a time out of me."

ROCK HEIGHTS

Selected heights* of some of rock's smallest and tallest stars.

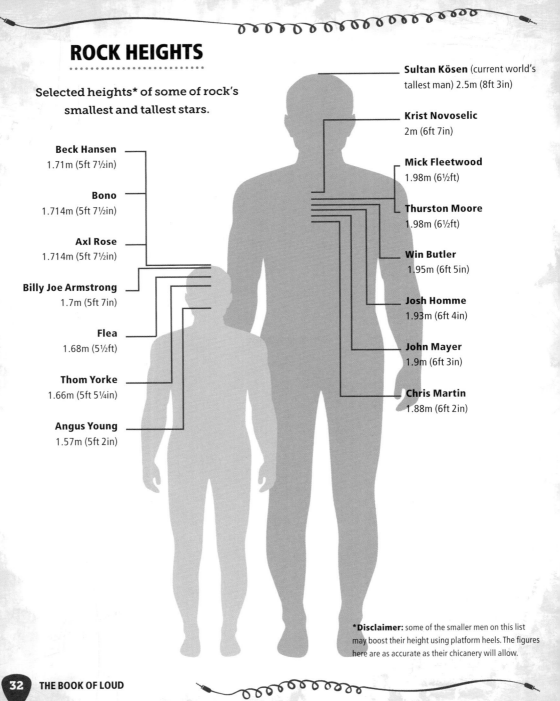

Sultan Kösen (current world's tallest man) 2.5m (8ft 3in)

Krist Novoselic
2m (6ft 7in)

Mick Fleetwood
1.98m (6½ft)

Thurston Moore
1.98m (6½ft)

Win Butler
1.95m (6ft 5in)

Josh Homme
1.93m (6ft 4in)

John Mayer
1.9m (6ft 3in)

Chris Martin
1.88m (6ft 2in)

Beck Hansen
1.71m (5ft 7½in)

Bono
1.714m (5ft 7½in)

Axl Rose
1.714m (5ft 7½in)

Billy Joe Armstrong
1.7m (5ft 7in)

Flea
1.68m (5½ft)

Thom Yorke
1.66m (5ft 5¼in)

Angus Young
1.57m (5ft 2in)

*Disclaimer: some of the smaller men on this list may boost their height using platform heels. The figures here are as accurate as their chicanery will allow.

ROCK HOTELS

....

Six legendary rock 'n' roll hotels you can check into,
plus one you can never leave.

HOTEL CHELSEA

222 West 23rd Street New York, New York, USA

Manhattan's Hotel Chelsea has drawn in many a rock
star since it opened in 1884. The residents' list is a who's
who of rock royalty, including the likes of Bob Dylan, Iggy
Pop, Pink Floyd, Ryan Adams, the Libertines and Anthony
Kiedis, many having celebrated its celebrity in song. But
having seen better days, it recently underwent significant
renovations designed to return its previous glamour.

www.chelseahotels.com

CHATEAU MARMONT

8221 Sunset Boulevard, Hollywood, California, USA

In what is becoming a theme, this Hollywood hotel is where
Led Zeppelin drove Harley Davidsons into the lobby, despite
there being ample parking opportunities outside. Jim
Morrison dangled from the hotel's windows, although he
pretty much did that everywhere, and various Red Hot Chili
Peppers have lived here at one time or another.

www.chateaumarmont.com

ANDAZ WEST HOLLYWOOD

8401 Sunset Boulevard
West Hollywood, California, USA

Legendarily, Led Zeppelin frequently resided here, and
the group's antics resulted in the place being nicknamed
the "Riot House". More recently, and more sedately, Kelly
Osbourne and Slipknot's Corey Taylor have stayed here.

www.westhollywood.hyatt.com

L'HOTEL

13 Rue des Beaux Arts, Paris, France

L'Hotel of many a libertine, The Doors' frontman Jim
Morrison called this place home for a while, though he
didn't die in the bathtub here, should your dark mind be
wondering – that was at an apartment elsewhere in the
city. Latterly, the likes of Lenny Kravitz have followed in his
footsteps – and without any drama.

www.l-hotel.com

HOTEL YORBA

4020 Lafayette Boulevard, Detroit, Michigan, USA

Fittingly, The White Stripes recorded their 2001 track *Hotel
Yorba* in one of the titular hotel's rooms. Open since 1923
but used more recently as a halfway house for felons, it
isn't the most salubrious hotel in this list (or in Detroit), but
you can, in theory, stay here. Just head for 4020 Lafayette
Boulevard and look up – the massive red capital-lettered
HOTEL YORBA sign makes it unmissable.

No website

HOTEL CALIFORNIA

Set off a dark desert highway, the precise location of Hotel
California is not specified – for the simple reason that it
doesn't actually exist. The hotel of the Eagles' imagination
was an allegory on hedonism and the American Dream. You
can check out any time you like, which is helpful, but you
can never leave, which is not.

www.eagles.com

THE ARTIST FORMERLY KNOWN AS...

Sometimes (well, often), rock stars are saddled with very regular,
non-rock, run-of-the-mill names.

ROCK STAR NAME	★	WAS...
David Bowie	★	David Robert Hayward Stenton Jones
John Mellor	★	Joe Strummer
Black Francis	★	Charles Thompson
Marilyn Manson	★	Brian Warner
Ozzy Osbourne	★	John Michael Osbourne
Iggy Pop	★	James Jewell Osterberg, Jr.
Lou Reed	★	Louis Firbank
Axl Rose	★	William Bruce Rose
Eric Clapton	★	Eric Patrick Clapp
Steven Tyler	★	Steven Talarico
Eddie Vedder	★	Edward Louis Severson
Jack White	★	John Anthony Gillis
Tré Cool	★	Frank Edwin Wright III
Flea	★	Michael Balzary
Sid Vicious	★	John Ritchie
Kid Rock	★	Robert Ritchie
Freddie Mercury	★	Farrokh Bulsara
Slash	★	Saul Hudson
Johnny Marr	★	John Maher
Buckethead	★	Brian Carroll
Courtney Love	★	Courtney Harrison
Henry Rollins	★	Henry Garfield

THE SPOTTER'S GUIDE :
THE GRUNGE KID

Here, learn how to spot that mainstay of the 1990s music scene, the grunge fan.

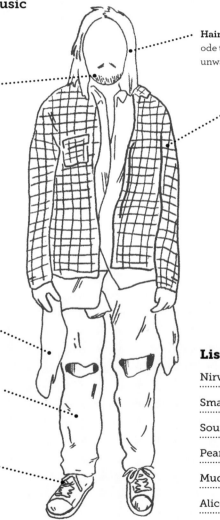

Hair shoulder-length in an ode to Kurt. Lank by nature, unwashed by design.

Stubbly goatee, usually kept just the right side of a full-blown beard.

Skinny frame bulked up using Cobain's Rule of Layering for clothing: three layers minimum, including plaid shirt and tatty band T-shirt.

Sweater. Despite Cobain's Rule of Layering, this is only ever worn around the waist for effect, never as the manufacturer actually intended it.

Jeans. Old, faded and loose enough to mosh around in.

Basketball shoes. Opts for a modest shade of black, dark blue or grey and worn to destruction.

Listening to:

Nirvana, *Nevermind*

Smashing Pumpkins, *Gish*

Soundgarden, *Superunknown*

Pearl Jam, *Ten*

Mudhoney, *Mudhoney*

Alice in Chains, *Dirt*

LONDON CALLING!

Navigating London's rock hotspots, one track at a time...

1.

For Tomorrow by **Blur** (1993)
In which the Essex four-piece find
themselves lost on the Westway – a stretch
of grey dual carriageway running from
Paddington to north Kensington.

2.

Battersea Odyssey
by **Super Furry Animals** (2007)
Concept album caper in which a character
named Venus moves from a small town to
the sprawling metropolis and discovers the
delights of Battersea, power station and all.

3.

Don't Go Back to Dalston
by **Razorlight** (2005)
Once full of drugs and danger, the Dalston
Johnny Borrell advised against returning
to is now full of hipsters with asymmetric
fringes and silly trousers.

4.

The Last Living Rose by **PJ Harvey** (2011)
In which the Dorset dame takes a walk
through the capital, down to the Thames River,
via stinking alleys and the music of drunken
violence. She went via Covent Garden, then.

12 The whole city

5.

Leicester Square by **Rancid** (1998)
Californian punk outfit take a trip to Blighty, then take a tube ride across London, only to find they are a long way from tourist hotspot Leicester Square. But that's no bad thing.

6.

Play With Fire by **The Rolling Stones** (1965)
The tale of a socialite's descent, from the splendour of Knightsbridge to the supposed slums of Stepney. A warning of what to expect if you mess with a Rolling Stone.

7.

Pentonville by **Babyshambles** (2005)
Reggae departure in which Pete Doherty recounts his spell in chokey, banged up at Her Majesty's pleasure in Pentonville nick. A building best viewed from the outside.

8.

Brompton Oratory
by **Nick Cave And The Bad Seeds** (1997)
Or to give it its full and grander title, The Church of the Immaculate Heart of Mary. Either way, this is one of London's most spectacular churches.

9.

Fake Plastic Trees by **Radiohead** (1995)
Another anthem of alienation, this time inspired by the fake greenery of the banking and business epicentre, Canary Wharf.

10.

The Fool On The Hill by **The Beatles** (1967)
Though Paul McCartney has since debunked the claim, it was said The Fool miraculously materialized before him on London's pleasant Primrose Hill, then disappeared as quickly as he arrived. Inspired, Macca wrote this song.

11.

22 Acacia Avenue by **Iron Maiden** (1982)
A tale of a lady of the night, peddling her wares in London's East End. The precise location of this Acacia Avenue is unclear, so don't go looking for her.

12.

London Calling by **The Clash** (1979)
Less a tourism campaign than an apocalyptic punk rock battle cry, spat angrily into the ether by Joe Strummer. Luckily, the "zombies of death" of 1979 are now long gone.

13.

The Guns of Brixton by **The Clash** (1979)
According to bassist Paul Simonon's account, this south London borough is full of guns and murderous intent. That was then though. Nowadays, it's slightly less terrifying.

14.

Waterloo Sunset by **The Kinks** (1967)
An ode to the time chief Kink Ray Davies was hospitalized in St Thomas', and the time he spent watching the world unfold below him as the dirty old Thames flowed gently by.

THE ARTISTS WHO SHAPED ROCK AND ROLL

To coincide with its opening in 1995, the Rock and Roll Hall of Fame created a list of *"500 Songs That Shaped Rock and Roll"*. Many, many artists made the list, but some popped up more often than most.

8 SONGS

THE BEATLES

A Day in the Life
HELP!
Hey Jude
I Want to Hold Your Hand
In My Life
Norwegian Wood
Strawberry Fields Forever
Yesterday

7 SONGS

ELVIS PRESLEY

Heartbreak Hotel
Hound Dog
Jailhouse Rock
Love Me Tender
Mystery Train
Suspicious Minds
That's All Right

6 SONGS

THE ROLLING STONES

Honky Tonk Women
(I Can't Get No) Satisfaction
Jumpin' Jack Flash
Miss You/Paint It Black
Sympathy for the Devil
Time Is on My Side

5 SONGS

BOB DYLAN

Blowin' in the Wind
Like a Rolling Stone
Subterranean Homesick Blues
Tangled Up in Blue
The Times They Are A-Changin'

LED ZEPPELIN

Dazed and Confused
Kashmir
Rock and Roll
Stairway to Heaven
Whole Lotta Love

CHUCK BERRY

Johnny B. Goode
Maybellene
Brown Eyed Handsome Man
Rock & Roll Music
Roll Over Beethoven

BRUCE SPRINGSTEEN

Born in the USA
Born to Run
Dancing in the Dark
Streets of Philadelphia
Rosalita (Come Out Tonight)

STEVIE WONDER/ LITTLE STEVIE WONDER

Fingertips
Living for the City
Master Blaster (Jammin')
Superstition
Uptight (Everything's Alright)

ROCK KNOWLEDGE
Pink Floyd's The Dark Side of the Moon holds the record for the longest period spent on Billboard's "Hot 200 Albums" list: 861 weeks, for 16 long years from 1973.

NOTABLE OTHER ONE-HIT WONDERS

Taken from the Rock and Roll Hall of Fame's "500 Songs That Shaped Rock and Roll".

Green Day
Basket Case

Guns N' Roses
Welcome to the Jungle

PJ Harvey
Dress

Jane's Addiction
Been Caught Stealin'

Metallica
Enter Sandman

My Chemical Romance
Welcome to the Black Parade

N.W.A.
F*ck tha Police

New Order
Blue Monday

Nine Inch Nails
Head Like a Hole

Radiohead
Karma Police

Red Hot Chili Peppers
Give It Away

Sonic Youth
Teenage Riot

The Sugarhill Gang
Rapper's Delight

Weezer
Undone (The Sweater Song)

HAMMERED!

When rock memorabilia walks in, sanity often walks out.

Elvis Presley's last prescription bottle – dated 15 August 1977 – sold for $800 (£558) in 2009. The King died the following day.

The Lucky Silver Dollar **Jimi Hendrix** kept on him at all times – which dated back to 1899 – sold for $2,641 (£1,840) in 2015.

The toaster **Elton John** received on his wedding day in 1984 sold for $1,062 (£740) in 2008. It was still in its original box.

Kurt Cobain's 1993 *"Unplugged"* sweater sold at auction in 2014 for $137,500 (£95,795).

In 2003, a London man attempted to sell the flu virus he claimed to have picked up from **Paul McCartney**. Listed on eBay, the bidding reached $1.83 (£1.28) before the item was removed.

Jerry Garcia's toilet, removed from the Grateful Dead main man's former home, sold in 2005 for $2,550 (£1,777).

A kitchen spoon once used and signed by **John Lennon** and **Yoko Ono** in 1969 was sold for $1,875 (£1,307) in 2008.

One of **John Lennon's** teeth sold for $27,984 (£19,500) in 2011, bought by a Canadian dentist who wants to clone the late Beatle.

A single piece of chewing gum discarded by Kiss frontman **Gene Simmons** sold in 2013 for $247,203 (£172,299) on eBay.

After **Moby** licensed every track on his *Play* album to advertising agencies, a former friend offered Moby's "eternal soul" on eBay in 2002. It sold for $42 (£29).

THEY FOUGHT THE LAW / THE LAW WON

KURT COBAIN

Having been arrested at age 18 on a count of vandalism in his home town of Aberdeen, Washington, in 1985, after having scrawled "Ain'T goT no how waTchamacalliT" on the side of a building, the future Nirvana frontman added another charge to his rap sheet after being caught trespassing while intoxicated on the roof of a local abandoned building. Cobain sat for the police mugshot but avoided jail time.

KISS THIS!

It has been predicted that since 1977, the total retail sales accumulated by the band Kiss have **exceeded $1 billion** (over £700 million). This excludes the money they make from their music or concert tickets, so that figure represents all the other stuff they sell or put their name to. Since 1973, the Kiss logo and name have been slapped on well over 3,000 products, ranging from the ridiculous to the preposterous. We're talking Kiss Kondoms, Kiss Him cologne and a quite essential Mount Kissmore, a 36 x 25cm (14 x 10in) carving of the four faces of Kiss on a solid stone rock face.

But Kiss are by no means alone in creating weird and wonderful merchandise. The list of bands attempting their own brand extensions is pretty impressive:

KISS Pinball machine

KISS Table lamp

KISS Monopoly board game

KISS Coffin

GWAR BBQ sauce

U2 Achtung Baby condoms

THE ROLLING STONES
Tongue and lips telephone

OK GO Air fresheners

MOTHER LOVE BONE Dog collar

OASIS-branded "Ar Kid" adidas trainers

THE RACONTEURS
Pure Consoling bath soap

THE WHITE STRIPES Sewing kit

ALICE COOPER Unisex mascara

METALLICA Pillowcase

THE FLAMING LIPS Silver Trembling Fetus Christmas tree ornament

AND, OF COURSE, THE MARSHALL FRIDGE

THE STYLE OF ROCK: *ROCK WHISKERS*

An artistic appreciation of rock's greatest face furniture.

THE HAMSTER ♟

Sported by Eagles of Death Metal frontman Jesse "The Devil" Hughes, this takes The Zappa and grows it out to look like a large rodent settling in for winter. It proves that, while the devil has all the best tunes, he doesn't necessarily have the best whiskers.

THE FREDDIE ♟

Longer than a Toothbrush, shorter than a Mexican, Freddie Mercury rocked a classic "chevron". Also beloved but never bettered by the likes of Ron Jeremy and Tom Selleck, with Freddie it sat atop a set of equally impressive teeth.

THE LEMMY ♟

The Lemmy connects moustache to sideburns via an otherwise hairless chin, technically making it more muttonchops than moustache. Facial hair fashions wax and wane, but The Lemmy remained a constant trademark of a rock life lived hard.

ROCK KNOWLEDGE

The only member of ZZ Top not to sport a long, lavish beard is, ironically, Frank Beard. But then he's the drummer, and drummers are different.

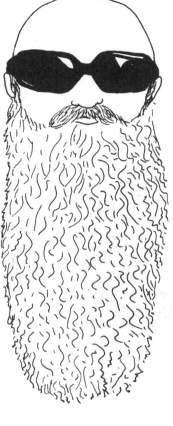

THE PRINCE OF DARKNESS ❦

A creation so admired it has its own social media following, Nick Cave has in truth made the most of a fairly average, wispy hand. Occasionally opting for the regulation "chevron", Cave is at his most impressive when embracing the full-on Horseshoe: essentially a goatee with a bare, barren, badass chin.

THE ZAPPA ❦

A Mexican up top, a soul patch below, the component parts here are more easily explained as a Zappa, in honour of Frank, a man as creative with a razor as with an axe.

THE ZZ TOP ⚡

In truth, one of rock's greatest examples of whiskerage owes much to man being basically bone idle. Both men returned from vacation unshaven and decided to let nature take its course. We should all be grateful for that.

12 BANNED RECORD COVERS

Band THE BEATLES 1966

Banned! The release of 1966's *Yesterday and Today* cover featured all four Beatles draped in dismembered (plastic) baby parts, which flew in the face of their previously wholesome image. As outrage ensued, 750,000 copies were recalled and the cover replaced with a safer, staged portrait of the band.

Band THE JIMI HENDRIX EXPERIENCE 1968

Banned! Hendrix filled the entire cover of his 1968 album *Electric Ladyland* with nubile and naked young ladies. It was too much for at least one UK record store, which refused to stock it until a safer alternative cover was provided.

Band PINK FLOYD 1975

Banned! *Wish You Were Here* featured a pair of businessmen shaking hands. The mild concern came from the fact that one of the men was on fire. It didn't bother him, but it bothered many shops, which refused to stock such corrupting images.

Band BON JOVI 1986

Banned! In 1986, Bon Jovi's original cover for breakthrough album *Slippery When Wet* featured a suggestive pair of lady's breasts barely contained by a wet T-shirt. Amid retail concerns, a safer black abstract theme was sourced and released – except in Japan, where the breasts were very popular.

Band JANE'S ADDICTION 1989

Banned! *Nothing's Shocking* claimed Jane's Addiction in 1989, but the cover of that album apparently was. It depicted a pair of naked, conjoined ladies with their heads on fire. Too shocking for many US stores, it was sold in a plain cover.

Band RED HOT CHILI PEPPERS 1989

Banned! The original cover for 1989's *Mother's Milk* fell foul of US censors which ruled the topless cover model was flashing too much flesh, despite the four Peppers being strategically placed to conceal her private parts. On the subsequent redesign, Keidis and Co. feature slightly bigger.

Band NIRVANA 1991

Banned! The depiction of a baby chasing a dollar in a swimming pool on the cover of *Nevermind* wasn't an issue for many US stores, so much as the fact you could see the little fella's little fella! The band appeased them by sticking a sticker over the offending appendage that read "*Featuring Smells Like Teen Spirit, Come As You Are, and Lithium*".

Band NIRVANA 1993

Banned! Back again. This time, having included the song *Rape Me* on the 1993 album *In Utero*, Nirvana kept the all-important supermarket chains happy by listing the track as *Waif Me* and removing all images of foetuses.

Band MARILYN MANSON 2000

Banned! Portraying himself as a crucified Christ with a missing jaw on the cover of 2000's *Holy Wood (In the Shadow of the Valley of Death)*, Marilyn Manson was provoking the censors. They bit back and banned the offending item – as he knew they would.

Band THE STROKES 2001

Banned! The Strokes' 2001 debut album *Is This It* featured the naked rear end of a female model, shot from the side and with sufficient suggestion to earn itself a ban. The black leather dominatrix-esque glove also didn't help. In the US, it was replaced by a psychedelic shot of subatomic particles.

Band MANIC STREET PREACHERS 2009

Banned! The cover to 2009's *Journal for Plague Lovers* featured a plague victim – too much for customers in several of Britain's leading supermarkets to handle, so it was sold behind a plain cover.

Band BAT FOR LASHES 2012

Banned! Natasha Khan's 2012 album *The Haunted Man* also fell foul of the supermarket chains: the sight of Khan naked but draped in a man whose limbs concealed her delicates earned itself a plain cover.

ROCK'S FINEST SUPERGROUPS

Warning: May Contain Traces of Dave Grohl

ATOMS FOR PEACE

2 Radiohead Thom Yorke – vocals, guitar
+ (Producer) Nigel Godrich – keyboards

+

2 Red Hot Chili Peppers Flea – bass
+ Mauro Refosco – percussion

+

1 Beck Joey Waronker – drums

Formed in 2009 and straddling the genres of experimental rock-dance-electronica, Atoms for Peace has so far released one album, 2013's *Amok*.

AUDIOSLAVE

1 Soundgarden Chris Cornell – vocals, guitar

+

3 Rage Against the Machine Tom Morello – guitar
+ Tim Commerford – bass + Brad Wilk – drums

Effectively, Rage Against the Machine without the frontman or the expletives. Audioslave formed in the early 2000s and released three albums: *Audioslave* (2002), *Out of Exile* (2005) and *Revelations* (2006).

CHICKENFOOT

2 Van Halen Sammy Hagar – vocals, guitar
+ Michael Anthony – bass

+

1 Joe Satriani Joe Satriani – guitar, keyboards

+

1 Red Hot Chili Pepper Chad Smith – drums

What started as a casual jam between Hagar, Anthony and Smith became a full-blown supergroup with the addition of perhaps the world's most gifted guitarist, Satriani. Their eponymous debut in 2009 was followed, in 2011, by the numerically confused *Chickenfoot III*.

CREAM

1 Yardbird Eric Clapton – guitar, vocals

+

2 Graham Bond Organisation Ginger Baker – drums
+ Jack Bruce – bass, vocals

Premier blues guitarist teams up with premier jazz drummer, adds equally gifted bassist and creates pioneering rock supergroup. Cream unleashed four gold and platinum albums in the space of three years. Reunions followed in the 1990s and 2000s.

THE DAMNED THINGS

2 Fall Out Boys Andy Hurley – drums
+ Joe Trohman – guitar

+

2 Anthrax Scott Ian – guitar
+ Rob Caggiano – guitar

+

2 Every Time I Die Keith Buckley – vocals
+ Josh Newton – bass

The Damned Things have so far released one album: 2010's *Ironiclast*.

THE DEAD WEATHER

1 White Stripe Jack White – drums, vocals, guitar

+

1 The Kills Alison Mosshart – guitar, vocals

+

1 Queen of the Stone Age Dean Fertita – guitar, keyboards

+

1 Raconteur Jack Lawrence – bass, drums

Founded in 2009 and still active, The Dead Weather released a debut album that year, *Horehound*. Two further albums followed: *Sea of Cowards* in 2010 and *Dodge and Burn* in 2015.

HOLLYWOOD VAMPIRES

6 Alice Cooper Alice Cooper – vocals + Tommy Henriksen – guitar + Dennis Dunaway – bass + Neal Smith – drums + Glen Sobel – drums + Kip Winger – bass

+

2 Hollywood Actors Johnny Depp – guitar + Christopher Lee (scary Dracula impressions)

+

3 Guns N' Roses Slash – guitar + Matt Sorum – drums + Duff McKagen – bass

+

2 Paul McCartneys Paul McCartney – guitar + Abe Laboriel, Jr. – drums

+

1 Aerosmith Joe Perry – guitar

+

1 Jane's Addiction Perry Farrell – vocals

+

1 Foo Fighter Dave Grohl – vocals, drums

+

1 AC/DC Brian Johnson – vocals

+

1 The Doors Robby Krieger – guitar

+

1 The Eagles Joe Walsh – guitar, vocals

+

1 The Who Zak Starkey – drums

+

1 Bruce Springsteen Bruce Witkin – multi-instrumentalist

+

1 Rage Against the Machine Tom Morello – guitar

+

1 Black Sabbath Geezer Butler – bass

+

1 Marilyn Manson Marilyn Manson – Marilyn Manson

Hollywood Vampires was formed in 2015 by Alice Cooper, Johnny Depp and Joe Perry, named after the legendary drinking club that gathered at the Rainbow Bar in LA and included Jim Morrison, Jimi Hendrix and Keith Moon. The collective is ever-changing, as guest musicians come and go. They have so far released one self-titled album (2015).

TEMPLE OF THE DOG

2 Soundgarden Chris Cornell – vocals + Matt Cameron – drums

+

4 Pearl Jam* Eddie Vedder – backing vocals + Stone Gossard – guitar + Jeff Ament – bass + Mike McCready – guitar

Formed in tribute to the late Mother Love Bone lead vocalist Andrew Wood, Temple of the Dog released one self-titled album, in 1991.

*A pedant will rightly point out that by this point, Pearl Jam hadn't actually formed. That would come shortly after and the album *Ten* was released a year later.

THEM CROOKED VULTURES

1 Queen of the Stone Age Josh Homme – lead vocals, lead and rhythm guitar

+

1 Foo Fighter Dave Grohl – drums, backing vocals

+

1 Led Zeppelin John Paul Jones – bass, keyboards, backing vocals

Formed in 2009 but talked about as far back as 2005, Them Crooked Vultures released a self-titled debut album in 2009. A second album has been in the pipeline since 2010 but has yet to see the light of day.

FFS

4 Franz Ferdinands Alex Kapranos – vocals, guitar + Nick McCarthy – guitar, keyboards + Bob Hardy – bass + Paul Thomson – drums

+

2 Sparks Ron Mael – keyboard + Russell Mael – vocals

Longstanding fans of one another, the Franz Ferdinand–Sparks mash-up goes back to the mid-2000s but the two only officially came together in 2014, releasing their eponymous debut album the following year.

LEGENDS OF LOUD
✳ ✳

In this series, we have chosen some of our favourite performers; the artists who embody the Marshall spirit. These are some of the true pioneers of rock – the Legends of Loud.

JIMMY PAGE
Classic Rock Riffmaster

The obvious analogy is with buildings. When it comes to creating songs, most guitarists build houses. Some of them build simple two-up, two-downs. Some spawn sprawling country estates with multiple rooms. Most create something in between. But Jimmy Page is very different.

With his music, Page builds cathedrals and superstructures of almost unimaginable ambition, scale and complexity. "My vocation is more in composition really than anything else," he once explained, "building up harmonies using the guitar, orchestrating the guitar like an army – a guitar army."

Those armies are legend. *In My Time of Dying*, *Dazed and Confused*, *When the Levee Breaks*, *Whole Lotta Love* and on, and on, and… Their output was formidable: quality and quantity. "To put out a greatest hits on one CD was totally impossible," reflected Page later. "The best compromise was to put out two CDs." But two barely did it justice.

In its prime, Led Zeppelin was hard rock's most dominant force, the most influential outfit of the 70s. The self-titled debut album had emerged in 1969, built and mixed in the space of nine days. It set the tone, breaking into America's *Billboard* Top 10 and shifting in the millions. Sales since then have been put at anywhere between 200 and 300 million; concert ticket sales have set numerous records along the way, their live performances becoming closer to religious rituals than simply four men making noise.

Jimmy Page is still building to this day, sticking impressively to the classic rock blueprint that served him so well originally. He may never create another building as mighty as those he created at the peak of his powers, but he doesn't need to. His work is done. His legend set in stone – built to last.

JOBBING ROCKERS

★★★

Sometimes, even rock royalty has to make ends meet.

ARTIST	★	BAND	★	WAS ONCE...
David Bowie	★	*	★	a butcher's delivery boy
Johnny Cash	★	*	★	a US Army military codebreaker
Kurt Cobain	★	Nirvana	★	a high school janitor
Jarvis Cocker	★	Pulp	★	a fishmonger's assistant, scrubbing crabs
Chris Cornell	★	Soundgarden	★	a fish handler for a seafood wholesaler
Roger Daltrey	★	The Who	★	a steelworker
Jonathan Davies	★	Korn	★	an undertaker
Debbie Harry	★	Blondie	★	a Playboy bunny at New York's Playboy Club
Mick Jagger	★	The Rolling Stones	★	a psychiatric hospital porter
Courtney Love	★	Hole	★	a stripper at Jumbo's Clown Room in LA
Brian May	★	Queen	★	an astronomer
Freddie Mercury	★	Queen	★	a market-stall owner at London's Kensington Market (selling art and clothes)
Morrissey	★	The Smiths	★	an Inland Revenue employee
Kele Okereke	★	Bloc Party	★	a cinema attendant
Ozzy Osbourne	★	*	★	a plumber, construction worker, slaughterhouse worker, morgue worker
Elvis Presley	★	*	★	a truck driver
Axl Rose	★	Guns N' Roses	★	paid to smoke cigarettes for medical research studies
Sting	★	The Police	★	a schoolteacher, tax officer, bus conductor
Joe Strummer	★	The Clash	★	a gravedigger
Eddie Vedder	★	Pearl Jam	★	a gas station security guard
Gerard Way	★	My Chemical Romance	★	a comic-book artist
Jack White	★	The White Stripes	★	a trainee priest and an upholsterer
Malcolm Young	★	AC/DC	★	a sewing machine mechanic in a bra factory

LESS IS MORE

Behold, the longest album title in rock.

PREVIOUSLY, IT HAD BEEN

When the Pawn Hits the Conflicts He Thinks like a King What He Knows Throws the Blows When He Goes to the Fight and He'll Win the Whole Thing 'fore He Enters the Ring There's No Body to Batter When Your Mind Is Your Might so When You Go Solo, You Hold Your Own Hand and Remember That Depth Is the Greatest of Heights and If You Know Where You Stand, Then You Know Where to Land and If You Fall It Won't Matter, Cuz You'll Know That You're Right.

by **Fiona Apple**, released in 1999.

UNTIL, IN 2008, BRITISH COMEDY BAND CHUMBAWUMBA RELEASED

The Boy Bands Have Won, and All the Copyists and the Tribute Bands and the TV Talent Show Producers Have Won, If We Allow Our Culture to Be Shaped by Mimicry, Whether from Lack of Ideas or from Exaggerated Respect. You Should Never Try to Freeze Culture. What You Can Do Is Recycle That Culture. Take Your Older Brother's Hand-Me-Down Jacket and Re-Style It, Re-Fashion It to the Point Where It Becomes Your Own. But Don't Just Regurgitate Creative History, or Hold Art and Music and Literature as Fixed, Untouchable and Kept Under Glass. The People Who Try to "Guard" Any Particular Form of Music Are, Like the Copyists and Manufactured Bands, Doing It the Worst Disservice, Because the Only Thing That You Can Do to Music That Will Damage It Is Not Change It, Not Make It Your Own. Because Then It Dies, Then It's Over, Then It's Done, and the Boy Bands Have Won.

THE FIRST 11 BANDS ON MTV

When it first appeared on our television sets at 12:01am on 1 August 1981, MTV (or Music Television as no one ever called it) heralded the birth of the music video, changing the way we consumed music forever. The first 11 songs played on MTV were a motley crew of the good, the bad and the downright ugly, and the list contained only a smattering of rock tracks.

1. *Video Killed the Radio Star*
   by The Buggles

2. *You Better Run*
   by Pat Benatar

3. *She Won't Dance with Me*
   by Rod Stewart

4. *You Better You Bet*
   by The Who

5. *Little Susie's on the Up*
   by Ph.D

6. *We Don't Talk Anymore*
   by Cliff Richard

7. *Brass in Pocket*
   by The Pretenders

8. *Time Heals*
   by Todd Rundgren

9. *Take It on the Run*
   by REO Speedwagon

10. *Rockin' the Paradise*
    by Styx

11. *When Things Go Wrong*
    by Robin Lane & The Chartbusters

The first Marshall amp, "Number One", was created in September 1962, the forerunner to the legendary JTM45. It now resides, behind glass, in the Marshall museum in Milton Keynes, England. Jim Marshall sold 23 of them the first day it went on sale.

JVM

Marshall

r to open

"HOLD ON THIS SOUNDS BETTER"

What classic albums were originally called...

BAND	★	ALBUM	★	WORKING TITLE
Arctic Monkeys	★	*AM*	★	*The New Black*
The Beatles	★	*Abbey Road*	★	*Everest*
Beck	★	*Midnight Vultures*	★	*Zatyricon/ I Can Smell the VD in the Club Tonite*
Blur	★	*Modern Life Is Rubbish*	★	*Britain vs. America*
The Clash	★	*London Calling*	★	*The Last Testament*
Fleetwood Mac	★	*Rumours*	★	*Don't Stop*
Green Day	★	*Dookie*	★	*Liquid Dookie*
Metallica	★	*Kill 'Em All*	★	*Metal Up Your Ass*
Nirvana	★	*In Utero*	★	*I Hate Myself and I Want to Die*
Nirvana	★	*Nevermind*	★	*Sheep*
Pink Floyd	★	*The Dark Side Of The Moon*	★	*Eclipse*
Pixies	★	*Doolittle*	★	*Whore*
Radiohead	★	*Hail to the Thief*	★	*The Gloaming/Little Man Being Erased/The Bony King of Nowhere/Snakes and Ladders*
The Rolling Stones	★	*Exile On Main St.*	★	*Tropical Disease*
The Smiths	★	*The Queen Is Dead*	★	*Margaret on the Guillotine*
U2	★	*Achtung Baby*	★	*Fear Of Women*
The Who	★	*Tommy*	★	*The Deaf, Dumb & Blind Boy*
Yeah Yeah Yeahs	★	*Show Your Bones*	★	*Coco Beware*

★ ROCK ★ KNOWLEDGE ★

During 1968 and 1969, Jimi Hendrix lived at 23 Brook Street in London. According to his girlfriend, Kathy Etchingham, he became a fan of British soap opera *Coronation Street* during this spell.

SCHOOL OF ROCK

How to... **Stage-dive**

WARNING: stage-diving should never be done unless the audience is receptive to it and the venue, the band and the security men allow you to stage-dive. If they don't, don't. But if they do...

FIG 1.
Clamber on the stage, which will be far easier in a smaller venue than at one of rock's enormo-domes. Choose your moment. You'll need to jump as the song is building up to the chorus or some crescendo, never during a quiet lull. And always act fast: you are not "The Show" and the longer you linger on stage, the higher the chance of you being ejected.

FIG 2.
Take a step back, aiming at a well-populated area of fans who look like they can ably take your weight and are willing to do so, then run toward the crowd.

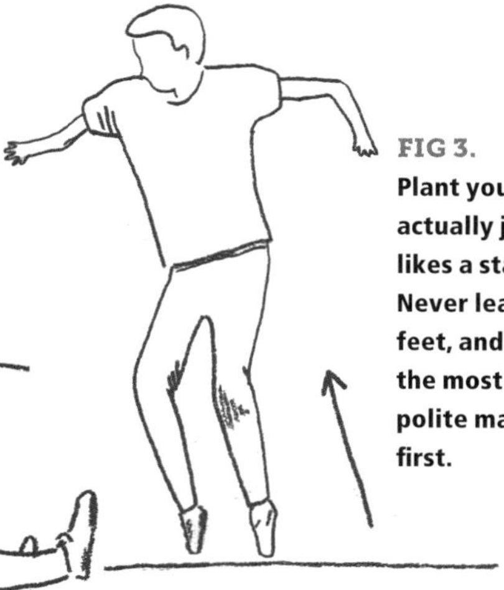

FIG 3.
Plant your foot and actually jump – nobody likes a stage-flopper. Never lead with your feet, and aim to land in the most comfortable, polite manner: back first.

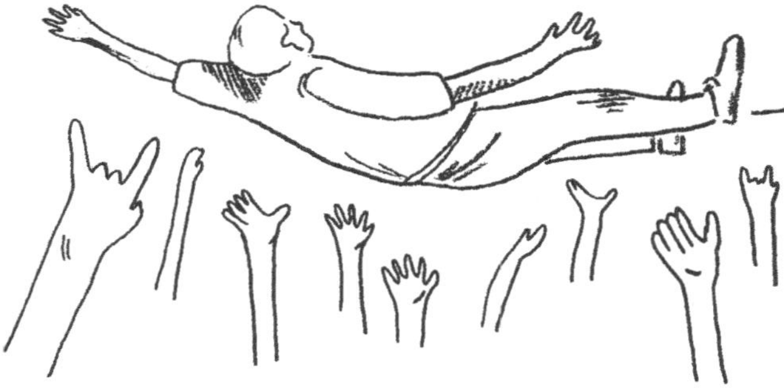

FIG 4.
Allow the crowd to swallow you up. Repeat if desired and your luck will hold.

ETYMOLOGY OF BAND NAMES

Often, inspiration strikes in the most unexpected places.

AC/DC

Legend has it that the young Young brothers spotted the letters of their future band on the side of their sister's sewing machine. The letters confirmed it could work on alternate and direct current.

ARCADE FIRE

Inspired by a story Win Butler heard as a child, from a bully who beat him up, that a local arcade had burned down and killed a number of kids.

BIFFY CLYRO

Unconfirmed but well worth recounting: it has been said that lead singer Simon Neil was once the proud owner of a Cliff Richard pen – a "Cliffy Biro". Creative spin took care of the rest.

BLACK REBEL MOTORCYCLE CLUB

One of two motorcycle gangs in the film *The Wild One*. That the other gang turned out to be The Beetles forced BRMC's hand somewhat.

THE DOORS

Inspired by Aldous Huxley's book *The Doors of Perception*, which quotes William Blake's "When the doors of perception are cleansed, things will appear to man as they truly are: infinite."

FOO FIGHTERS

Dave Grohl took inspiration from a World War II term for UFOs and other unexplained flying phenomena. "It's the stupidest f*cking band name in the world," rued Grohl, years later.

FALL OUT BOY

Performing without a name for its first two shows, the band opened it up to the audience, one of whom suggested the sidekick of *The Simpsons'* comic-book superhero Radioactive Man.

GUNS N' ROSES

Tracii Guns of L.A. Guns forms band with Axl Rose of Hollywood Rose. They combine the names and the rest you know.

THE JAM

Gifted to Modfather Paul Weller by his sister, who reportedly turned to him at breakfast and remarked that, while there was a band called Bread, there was not one called Jam.

THE KILLERS

Watch New Order's video for the song *Crystal* and you'll see a fictitious band performing. That band was named The Killers, and Brandon Flowers was taking note.

LED ZEPPELIN

Discussing plans to form a rock supergroup, Keith Moon and John Entwistle remarked that the idea would go down like a lead balloon – i.e. be a disaster. They changed the spelling of Led to ensure correct pronunciation.

LINKIN PARK

Forced to change their name for copyright issues, lead singer Chester Bennington wanted the name of the local Lincoln Park. He settled on a variant spelling.

MARILYN MANSON

The satanic love child of Hollywood bombshell Marilyn Monroe and deranged cult leader Charles Manson.

MY CHEMICAL ROMANCE

Said to have been inspired by the title of Irvine Welsh's *Ecstasy: Three Tales of Chemical Romance*.

NIRVANA

An attempt to transcend the cycle of human rebirth and human suffering was said to be behind the choice of band name for Kurt Cobain, for whom the earlier option of "Ted, Ed, Fred" just didn't quite cut it.

PIXIES

Guitarist Joey Santiago chose the name at random when flicking through the pages of a dictionary. The band reputedly liked the word's definition of "mischievous little elves".

PORNO FOR PYROS

Perry Farrell's post-Jane's Addiction outfit was inspired by the Los Angeles riots of 1992, when large swathes of the city were set ablaze during looting.

THE PRODIGY

The name here was partly inspired by main man Liam Howlett's first synthesizer, a Moog Prodigy.

QUEENS OF THE STONE AGE

A name devised by producer Chris Goss, Josh Homme stated that it was "heavy enough for the boys and sweet enough for the girls".

THE VELVET UNDERGROUND

Inspired by Michael Leigh's book of the same name, a lighthearted little tome on sadomasochism.

WEEZER

Named after the nickname given to him as an asthmatic child, Rivers Cuomo needed the name when his unnamed band was invited to open for Keanu Reeves' band Dogstar in 1992.

ANATOMY OF... AN ELECTRIC GUITAR

But remember, no *Stairway to Heaven*...

TUNERS
Geared mechanisms raise and lower tension of the strings, changing the pitch. The strings wrap tight around the protruding posts.

NUT
Stiff nylon strip that stops the strings vibrating beyond the neck.

BRIDGE
Metal plate that anchors the strings to the body.

BAR
A metal rod sometimes attached to the bridge that varies the string tension by tilting the bridge back and forth.

FINGERBOARD
(Also called fretboard.) This contains frets: thin metal bars running perpendicular to the strings that shorten the vibrating length of a string, controlling different pitches.

PICKUPS
Magnets that create the electrical current, which the amplifier converts into sweet rock sounds.

NECK
The long, club-like wooden piece that connects the headstock to the body.

STRINGS
The business end of any guitar. Designed to be twanged.

VOLUME AND TONE CONTROLS
These vary the volume and the guitar's bass and treble frequencies.

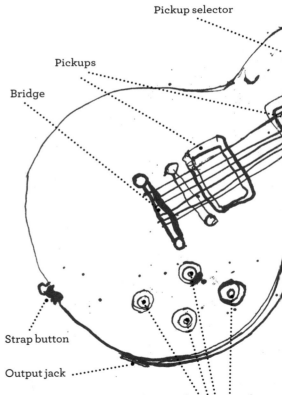

Pickup selector

Pickups

Bridge

Strap button

Output jack

Volume and tone controls

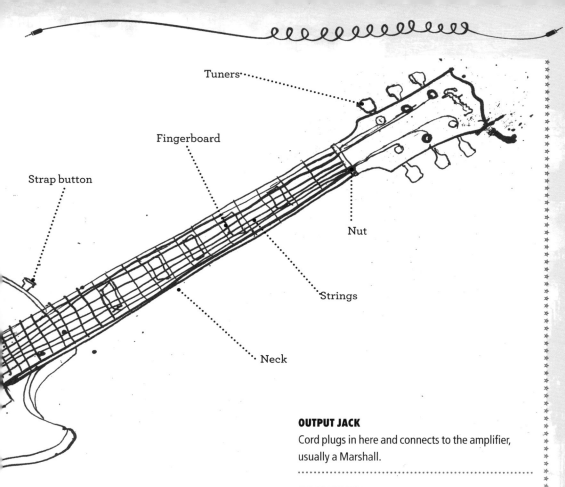

Tuners

Fingerboard

Strap button

Nut

Strings

Neck

OUTPUT JACK
Cord plugs in here and connects to the amplifier, usually a Marshall.

STRAP BUTTON
Without this, the strap would not be secure and the guitar would fall to the floor.

PICKUP SELECTOR
Switches between pickups to determine which is active.

"LET'S GET THE BAND BACK TOGETHER!"

Rock history is littered with bands that split and reform.
Some, however, take far longer than others.

1982	1987	
The Who		**5 years**

2004	2010	
The Libertines		**6 years**

2000	2008	
Rage Against The Machine		**8 years**

1994	2005	
Pink Floyd		**11 years**

1997	2010	
Soundgarden		**13 years**

1980	1994	
The Eagles		**14 years**

1996	2011	
The Stone Roses		**15 years**

1986	2007	
The Police		**21 years**

1968	2005	
Cream		**27 years**

ROCK ★ KNOWLEDGE

The only artist inducted three times into the Rock and
Roll Hall of Fame is Eric Clapton, for his slow-handed
wizardry in The Yardbirds (inducted 1992) and Cream
(1993), and for his solo endeavours (2000). A whole
litany of rock royalty are two-time inductees, including
Lou Reed, Jimmy Page and Neil Young, plus all four of
The Beatles.

THE ANIMALS

* *

A brief and very selective history of rock stars and their pets…

The rock-star pet of choice appears, by some distance, to be the faithful hound.

Jim Morrison had his labrador, Sage, **Steven Tyler** carries his Yorkie–Maltese crossbreeds around with him everywhere, while **Elvis Presley** had all manner of hound dogs down the years, including Baba, Edmund, Getlo, Muffin, Stuff, Sweat Pea, Foxhugh. Bush frontman **Gavin Rossdale** immortalised Winston, his massive Hungarian sheepdog, by sticking his photograph on the back cover of their debut album, *Sixteen Stone*, while **Elton John's** cocker spaniel Arthur served as best man at his civil partnership ceremony with David Furnish. Reformed hell-raiser and bat botherer **Ozzy Osbourne** owned Japanese Chin breed Maggie and Pomeranian Little Bit, which ended up being eaten by a coyote in the Hollywood hills. Led Zeppelin's **Robert Plant** named his hound Strider, inspired by Aragorn in J.R.R. Tolkien's *Lord of the Rings* trilogy. Perhaps the most celebrated rock hound of all was **Eric Clapton's** Weimaraner, Jeep. As well as appearing on the cover of Clapton's long-player *There's One In Every Crowd*, Jeep was celebrated in song on George Harrison's *I Remember Jeep*, an instrumental on the album *All Things Must Pass*. Similarly, **Paul McCartney's** trusty Old English sheepdog Martha received a nod on the *White Album* on the track *Martha My Dear*.

Cats are almost as popular. Both **John Lennon** and **McCartney** had cats named Jesus. Lennon also had Major and Minor. **Billy Corgan** name two of his Mister Thom and Miss Samm, while **Frank Zappa** kept up his tradition of bat-shit-crazy names with Fighty-Bitey and Marshmoff. Meanwhile **Freddie Mercury** had a number of moggies during his life, including Delilah, which he paid tribute to with a song of the same name on Queen's album *Innuendo*, in which the feline star pissed all over his Chippendale suite.

Finally, thankfully, there is some evidence of proper rock-star pets. Both **Alice Cooper** and **Slash** have pet snakes; Cooper's many snakes have popped up in his performances – the likes of Cobra Winfrey, Count Strangula and Julius Squeezer. His latest model, Christopher, is named after the late actor Christopher Lee. Slash's boa constrictor was named Pandora and appeared in the video to *Patience*. Meanwhile, **Elvis** again, while he never owned a snake, he did once have a pet kangaroo, a pet turkey named Bowtie and a beer-drinking chimp named Scatter.

THE SPOTTER'S GUIDE :
THE GOTH

Here, learn how to spot the
embodiment of darkness,
the goth.

**Face piercings and
tattoos** are entirely
optional but often
applauded.

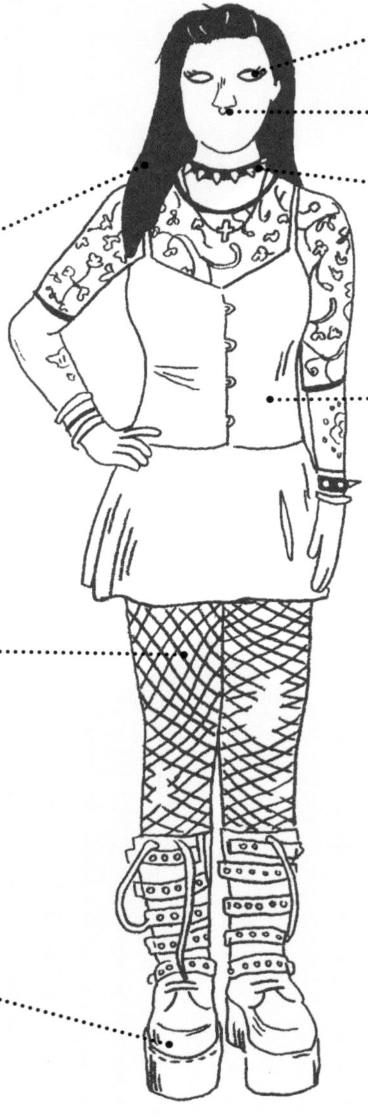

Hair a satanic shade of black, either by
nature or through the use of chemicals.
Purple or red streaks and shaved sides are
entirely optional.

The tight black jeans are tight
and black. Viable alternatives
include PVC bondage leggings
or fishnets, preferably ripped.

The shoes are always boots. Large,
well-heeled, big-buckled, clumpy boots
which must only be black. Always.

Aversion-to-sunlight white face, embellished with eyeliner for her and guyliner for him.

Dog collar. Extra points for cross, double points for spikes.

One-size-fits-all corset: his and hers, always black and always painfully tight. A band T-shirt is a viable alternative, but again, it must be black and it must be suffocatingly tight.

Listening to:

The Cure, *Standing on a Beach*

Sisters of Mercy, *First and Last and Always*

The Mission, *Children*

Alien Sex Fiend, *Acid Bath*

London After Midnight, *Psycho Magnet*

Gene Loves Jezebel, *The House of Dolls*

Inkubus Sukkubus, *Wytches*

THE MOST ICONIC SONG OF ALL TIME?

According to a study by researchers at Goldsmiths, University of London, the most iconic song of all time is officially, scientifically **Nirvana's *Smells Like Teen Spirit***. By studying seven "all-time best" lists from music critics, the boffins were able to run each track through analytical software to compare a variety of characteristics, including the song's key, beats per minute, chord variety, lyrical content and sonic variance. They undermined their complicated algorithm by stating that the key is simply to write the most different, diverse and exciting song possible, but helpfully listed the top 50 of all time.

THE TOP FIVE READ:

1.
SMELLS LIKE TEEN SPIRIT
by Nirvana

2.
IMAGINE
by John Lennon

3.
ONE
by U2

4.
BILLIE JEAN
by Michael Jackson

5.
BOHEMIAN RHAPSODY
by Queen

BLACKLISTED

* *

A brief history of songs that fell foul of the censors.

MY GENERATION (1965)
The Who
The Outrage! The BBC deemed that Roger Daltrey's stuttering lines could cause offence to listeners who had stutters.

. . . .

LET'S SPEND THE NIGHT TOGETHER (1967)
The Rolling Stones
The Outrage! The saucy Stones were clearly promoting promiscuity, which irked US TV host Ed Sullivan so much he made them change the lyric to "Let's spend some time together". The band later returned to the stage in Nazi uniforms, earning themselves a two-year ban from the show.

. . . .

LIGHT MY FIRE (1967)
The Doors
The Outrage! Also appearing on *Ed Sullivan*, The Doors had agreed to change the line "Girl, we couldn't get much higher", to "Girl, we can't get much better". Jim Morrison reneged and sang it anyway, with gusto.

. . . .

LUCY IN THE SKY WITH DIAMONDS (1967)
The Beatles
The Outrage! It was thought to contain drug references, most notably in the LSD title. The band denied the claims, though Paul McCartney later admitted the reference was "pretty obvious".

. . . .

LOLA (1970)
The Kinks
The Outrage! This time, a line referring to Coca-Cola violated the BBC's strict anti-advertising policy. It was later changed to cherry cola, at great cost to the band.

. . . .

GOD SAVE THE QUEEN (1977)
Sex Pistols
The Outrage! Unsurprisingly, this was pulled by the BBC for its anti-monarchy sentiments, particularly the refrain "God save the Queen, the facist regime".

. . . .

ATOMIC (1979)
Blondie
The Outrage! One of 67 songs deemed inappropriate and blacklisted by the BBC at the time of the Persian Gulf War, 1990–91.

. . . .

JEREMY (1991)
Pearl Jam
The Outrage! Setting the issue of teen suicide to a catchy tune, Jeremy was banned in the US in the aftermath of school shootings in the country.

COP KILLER (1992)
Body Count
The Outrage! Well, it was a song about killing policemen...

DISARM (1993)
Smashing Pumpkins
The Outrage! Billy Corgan and Co. were prevented from playing their seemingly innocent track on the BBC's *Top of the Pops* because of the line "cut that little child".

SMACK MY BITCH UP (1997)
The Prodigy
The Outrage! The misinterpreted misogynistic lyrics saw this one blacklisted by the BBC, though it later allowed a lyric-free version to be aired.

LEARN TO FLY (1999)
Foo Fighters
The Outrage! This was one of many tracks blacklisted by radio stations in the US in the aftermath of the terrorist attacks on 11 September 2001.

HASH PIPE (2001)
Weezer
The Outrage! Banned by the BBC's Radio One for what it believed was the promotion of an illegal substance.

AMERICAN IDIOT (2004)
Green Day
The Outrage! Though never actually banned, the band was forced to change the lyric "Maybe I am the faggot America" to "Maybe I am the sound of America".

PAPER PLANES (2007)
M.I.A.
The Outrage! The sound of gunshot during the chorus led to censorship on MTV and during an appearance on the US talk show Late Night with David Letterman.

NOTE: In many cases, particularly in recent years, songs considered to be offensive were not added to any official blacklist. They were simply deprived of any airtime.

FIGHT CLUB!

Rock music's most entertaining altercations.

PAUL MCCARTNEY
Vs
JOHN LENNON

When The Beatles split in 1970, the poster boys began to feud, first sniping via the press, then later trading insults via their musical output. In 1971, Macca's *Too Many People* ridiculed Lennon's armchair politics – "Too many people preaching practices," he sang. "Don't let 'em tell you what you wanna be." Lennon hit back with *How Do You Sleep?*, which contained the line: "Those freaks was right when they said you was dead." (see page 17). The friction faded and the pair worked together again, but relations were strained right up to Lennon's murder in 1980.

ROCK KNOWLEDGE

The Ramones took their name from Paul Ramon – the name Paul McCartney used when checking into hotels with The Silver Beatles.

ANTHONY KIEDIS
Vs
MIKE PATTON

When the Red Hot Chili Peppers frontman first clocked the video for Faith No More's 1990 hit *Epic*, he accused FNM frontman Mike Patton of ripping off his style. (There was even talk of Kiedis kidnapping the brazen upstart and chopping off his foot, but that was just jest, and Patton remains dual-footed to this day.) A little press-based verbal exchange ensued, but the squabble soon died down, only to flare up again in 1999, when Kiedis allegedly had Patton's Mr. Bungle pulled from the Big Day Out festival in Australia, and Patton and Co. responded by ridiculing Kiedis for being a former heroin addict. The beef seemingly remains strong to this day.

COURTNEY LOVE
Vs
DAVE GROHL

Asked to name his favourite song of Love's during an interview with Howard Stern, Grohl selected *Teenage Whore*: "Because I know she wrote it." And so began one of Love's many feuds, with Kurt's widow going on to accuse Mr Foo of numerous crimes, including stealing money from her and propositioning the now-adult daughter she had with Cobain, a claim Grohl vehemently denied. The two finally patched up their differences during Nirvana's induction into the Rock and Roll Hall of Fame in 2014. "It's time to make amends," said Love.

THE EAGLES
★ ☆ **Vs** ☆ ★
THE EAGLES

Tensions tore at the Eagles toward the end of the 70s, a decade in which all they touched had turned to gold discs. Things reached a head on stage in Long Beach in 1980, when singer Glenn Frey and guitarist Don Felder spent the evening at each other's throats. As the gig drew to a close, Felder turned to the frontman and yelled: "Only three more songs until I kick your ass, pal!" The band finally split soon after, and when Don Henley was later asked when they would re-form, he replied: "When hell freezes over". When they reunited to tour in 1994, the live album that followed was titled: *Hell Freezes Over*.

KID ROCK
★ ☆ **Vs** ☆ ★
TOMMY LEE

Given that both were married to Pamela Anderson at some point, it was inevitable that tensions which had been simmering nicely for years between Rock and Lee finally boiled over at the 2007 MTV Video Music Awards. After a bit of verbal jousting, Rock knocked the Mötley Crüe drummer's hat off before punching him near the face. Security stepped in and spoiled the show, but Lee later responded, bravely, via his website, by referring to Rock as "Kid Pebble". The two have since apologized and are now on better terms.

TRENT REZNOR
★ ☆ **Vs** ☆ ★
MARILYN MANSON

A shared love of the dark side had brought Reznor and Manson together, with the Nine Inch Nails man producing Manson's *Antichrist Superstar* and signing him up to his Nothing Records label. When the little satanist left to join Interscope in the late 90s, however, the wheels came off. NIN's *Starf*ckers* was said to have been written with Manson in mind. He responded by saying: "I think fame and power distort people's personalities." The two later made up, performing the very same song on stage at Madison Square Garden.

In this series, we have chosen some of our favourite performers; the artists who embody the Marshall spirit. These are some of the true pioneers of rock – the Legends of Loud.

KAREN O
The Queen of New York

Karen Orzolek is the classic rock chameleon, a riddle wrapped in a mystery, inside an enigma… hidden behind a fringe and dressed on just about the right side of insanity. Born in South Korea in 1978 but soon transplanted in New Jersey, Orzolek would later become O and formed folk-rock duo Unitard with guitarist Nick Zinner in Manhattan in 2000. They added a drummer and went electric and the Yeah Yeah Yeahs were born. And while the world didn't need another guitar band back then, the world didn't realize that it really did need Karen O.

From dive bar openers for The White Stripes and The Strokes, the Yeah Yeah Yeahs ascended rapidly, their debut EP leading to a record-company bidding war. But their reputation was being built on live shows, where Karen O hogged the stage and the limelight. A prowling, squawking, pulsating presence at the centre of everything, she brought energy, intensity and insanity, lying flat on her back and spraying beer from her mouth into the crowd. "You have to open up on stage," she says, with a fine line in understatement. But it's all just an act. "My onstage persona really is a persona," she says. Sixteen years and four albums later, it's hard to know who the real Karen O might be. In that time the Yeah Yeah Yeahs have jumped effortlessly from garage-punk to electro-dance, via gospel, fuzz-rock and heartbreaking balladry with effortless ease. And at the centre of it all stands Karen O, though never just standing still. It may all just be an act. But no one does it better.

ROCK 'N' ROLL GUACAMOLE!

★★★

In 2015, Jack White's rider for a gig in Oklahoma was made public. His management company was furious that private information had been released, but for fans of guacamole in particular, it was great news. Jack's instructions were as follows:

8 large, ripe Haas avocados (cut in half the long way, remove the pit – SAVE THE PITS THOUGH – and dice into large cubes with a butter knife, 3 or 4 slits down, 3 or 4 across. You'll scoop out the chunks with a spoon, careful to maintain the avocado in fairly large chunks.)

4 vine-ripened tomatoes, diced

Half a yellow onion, finely chopped

1 full bunch cilantro (fresh coriander), chopped

1 Serrano peppers, de-veined and chopped

1 lime

Salt and pepper to taste

Mix all the ingredients in a large bowl, careful not to mush the avocados too much. We want it chunky. Once properly mixed and tested, add the pits into the guacamole and even out the top with a spoon or spatula. Add half a lime to the top layer so you cover most of the surface with the juice. (The pits and lime will keep it from browning prematurely.) Cover with plastic wrap and refrigerate until served. Please don't make it too early before it's served. We'd love to have it around 5pm.

NOTE: Jack White's management moved quickly to stress that the artist doesn't actually write his own rider. But even so, it's a good recipe.

★ ★

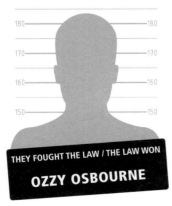

THEY FOUGHT THE LAW / THE LAW WON

OZZY OSBOURNE

Rock legend infamously has it that the Prince of Darkness was arrested for urinating on a wall of the historic Alamo after a show in San Antonio, Texas, in 1982 – but on this occasion rock legend is wrong.

The legendary Black Sabbath frontman was actually across the road, beside a 18-m (60-ft) monument that commemorates the Battle of the Alamo, but he was urinating – and wearing one of his wife, Sharon's, dresses.

He was arrested, charged with public intoxication and banned from performing in San Antonio for 10 years.

ROCK ARTISTS WITH THE MOST ALBUM CERTIFICATIONS

****

That's official jargon for whose releases have earned them the most discs in the UK.

ARTIST	GOLD	PLATINUM	MULTIPLATINUM	DIAMOND	TOTAL
Elvis Presley	90	52	25	1	168
The Beatles	48	42	26	6	122
The Rolling Stones	43	28	11	1	83
Aerosmith	25	18	12	1	56
Led Zeppelin	19	18	14	5	56
AC/DC	22	20	12	1	55
Bob Dylan	33	15	5	0	53
Alabama	22	20	10	0	52
Bruce Springsteen	22	17	10	2	51
Chicago	23	18	8	0	49
Pink Floyd	19	15	12	2	48
U2	23	11	7	1	42

THE GOLD (AND PLATINUM) STANDARD

★ ★

If a band or act sells enough records, CDs or digital tracks, they are awarded a nice commemorative framed disc. The volume of sales determines the standard of disc, but this varies slightly, depending on the country.

BRITISH PHONOGRAPHIC INDUSTRY

DISC AWARDED	SINGLES	ALBUMS
Silver	200,000	60,000
Gold	400,000	100,000
Platinum	600,000	300,000
Multiplatinum	Multiples of 600,000	Multiples of 300,000

RECORDING INDUSTRY ASSOCIATION OF AMERICA

DISC AWARDED	SINGLES	ALBUMS	DIGITAL SINGLES
Gold	500,000+	500,000+	500,000+
Platinum	1,000,000+	1,000,000+	1,000,000+
Double-Platinum		2,000,000+	
Multiplatinum	2,000,000+	3,000,000+	2,000,000+

★ ★

THEY FOUGHT THE LAW / THE LAW WON

BOB DYLAN

If a man can't take a walk in the rain without being apprehended on suspicion of being an escapee from the local mental hospital, what has the world come to? Back in 2009, rock royalty Bob Dylan took a stroll through Long Branch, New Jersey, killing time while on tour, dressed in two raincoats and with his trousers tucked into his boots. Local residents reported an "eccentric-looking old man" to police, who swooped and discovered he had no ID. Back on his nearby tour bus, a flash of Dylan's passport was enough to avert any charges.

ROCK ★ KNOWLEDGE

Search for a video of the Inspiral Carpets' performance at the Reading Festival in 1990 and you'll see a pantomime cow walk onto the stage. One half of that cow was Noel Gallagher, back then a roadie for the band.

ROCK ★ KNOWLEDGE

Before he renamed himself Bob Dylan and established himself as one of the most important performers in rock music history, Robert Allen Zimmerman briefly went by the name of Elston Gunn.

In 1989, the US military blasted out AC/DC music at General Manuel Noriega's compound in Panama for two continuous days. After 48 hours of this aural onslaught, the dictator duly surrendered.

Before joining Guns N' Roses, Slash had auditioned for hair-metal outfit Poison and made it to the final two. He decided against joining when he was asked if he'd be prepared to wear make up, thus changing the course of hard-rock history for ever.

The Who's certifiable drummer Keith Moon had a habit of blowing up hotel toilets using fireworks – what he called a "cherry bomb". For some reason, it led to him being banned for life from the Holiday Inn, Sheraton and Hilton chains.

Hard-living Rolling Stones guitarist Keith Richards has named his tipple of choice "Nuclear Waste". It contains two parts premium vodka, one ounce of Sunkist, or any orange soda and plenty of ice. "Lovely," says Keith.

SCHOOL OF ROCK

How to... Perform a Rock Salute

The rock salute has been used since time immemorial, particularly when listening to the heavier end of the musical spectrum. You may know it as the "devil horns", or just that funny pointy-fingers thing, but either way, mastering the technique is as essential as it is easy. So…

FIG 1.
Choose a hand, any hand, and extend it in front of you, holding all your digits out straight.

FIG 2.
Fold your middle and ring fingers into the palm of your hand, then curve your thumb around to cover them.

FIG 3.
Proudly extend your new "rock arm" above your head and begin banging your head up and down in time with the music. Repeat until the music stops – or your head starts to hurt.

"ABSOLUTELY NO BROWN ONES"

The truth behind Van Halen's legendary rider

The most legendary rock rider of them all was written in 1982, penned by Van Halen or a member of the group's management. The full document is way too long to condense here, but it contained the now infamous "M&M demand". The abridged version read: *"One case of Budweiser beer, four cases of Schlitz Malt Liquor beer (16-ounce cans), three fifths of Jack Daniel's Black Label bourbon, two fifths of Stolichnaya vodka, one pint of Southern Comfort, two bottles of Blue Nun white wine, herring in sour cream, one large tube of KY Jelly and M&M's (WARNING: ABSOLUTELY NO BROWN ONES)".*

We'll gloss over why they wanted KY Jelly and focus on the M&Ms – a request which suggested that a new level of egomania was at play. Legend had it that if Van Halen frontman Dave Lee Roth entered the dressing room and spotted a brown M&M, the backstage area got trashed. The truth was far from that.

The band's "M&M clause" was written into the contract for a very specific purpose. Buried away among pages of complicated technical instruction, it stated: *"There will be no brown M&M's in the backstage area, upon pain of forfeiture of the show, with full compensation."*

The reasoning was that if Dave Lee Roth did arrive backstage and spot a brown M&M, he'd know instantly that the contract hadn't been read properly. And if the contract hadn't been read properly, technical problems would almost certainly follow during the show. In other words, the brown M&Ms were not a symbol of rampant excess, rather an early warning tripwire that set alarm bells ringing.

FOOL'S GOLD LOAF

How to make Elvis Presley's favourite snack.

Like no other rock star before or since, Elvis Presley embraced a life of epicurean excess – including the now-famous Fool's Gold Loaf. This consists of a hollowed-out loaf of bread, filled with very generous layers of peanut butter, jelly, and bacon. The precise quantities remain in question but the basic ingredients are as follows:

1 LOAF OF BREAD
1 JAR OF PEANUT BUTTER (CRUNCHY OR SMOOTH)
1 JAR OF JELLY (THAT'S JAM, TO THE BRITISH)
1 LB OF BACON
1 TUB OF BUTTER

METHOD

Preheat the oven to 350˚F/180˚C.

Slice the loaf in half lengthwise, slather all over with butter, then brown it in the oven.

While the bread is browning, fry the bacon and drain it on paper towels (kitchen paper).

Hollow out the loaf's interior to make space for the rest of the ingredients.

Apply a thick layer of peanut butter in the base of the hollowed-out loaf.

Apply thick layer of jelly on top of the peanut butter.

Add the bacon. All of it.

Add the top of the loaf and eat.

NOTE: serves as many as 10 – or as few as 1 Elvis.

ROCK ★ KNOWLEDGE

Before hitting pay dirt as Elvis Presley's agent, Colonel Tom Parker ran a troupe of dancing chickens: "Col. Parker and His Amazing Dancing Chickens". He made them dance by concealing a hotplate beneath their feet.

THE STYLE OF ROCK: *ROCK FOLLICLES*

Rock-star haircuts come in a wide range of styles, though they never veer too far from these classic cuts.

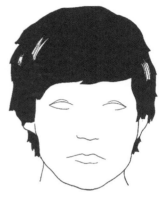

THE MOPTOP

Prime exponents: The Beatles, Ian Brown, Clint Boon, Noel Gallagher

THE LONG & LUSTROUS / LONG & LANK

Prime exponents: Anthony Kiedis, Axl Rose, Kid Rock, Dave Grohl, Nathan Followill (Kings of Leon) *Joshua Tree*-era Bono

THE CURLS

Prime exponents: Robert Plant, Jim Morrison, Roger Daltrey, Slash

THE DREADS

Prime exponents: Zack de la Rocha, Lenny Kravitz, Mike Bordin (Faith No More), Brandon Boyd (Incubus)

THE MOD

Prime exponents: Steve Marriott (Small Faces), Paul Weller, Liam Gallagher

THE CURTAINS

Prime exponents: Kurt Cobain, Beck, Jeff Buckley, Gerard Way (My Chemical Romance), Caleb Followill (Kings of Leon), Julian Casablancas

THE QUIFF

Prime exponents: Elvis, Johnny Marr, Josh Homme, Alex Turner, Mark Ronson

THE MANY GENRES OF METAL

It's a well-known fact that there are almost as many genres of metal as there are bands.
Here's a quick reference guide to help us get a handle on rock's darker oeuvre.

BLACK METAL = **HEAVY METAL + TEMPO + SHRIEKING VOCALS + DISTORTED GUITARS**
Prime examples: Mayhem, Darkthrone, Venom

DEATH CORE = **DEATH METAL + METALCORE + HARDCORE PUNK**
Prime examples: Antagony, Despised Icon, Bring Me the Horizon

DEATH METAL = **VERY VERY HEAVY METAL + DISTORTION**
Prime examples: Venom, Slayer, Aborted

DOOM METAL = **VERY HEAVY METAL + SLOWER TEMPO**
Prime examples: Pentagram, Witchfinder General, Cathedral

FOLK METAL = **HEAVY METAL + PAGANISM + BANJO + UKULELE**
Prime examples: Finntroll, Ensiferum, Ulver

FUNK METAL = **ALTERNATIVE METAL + HEAVY METAL + FUNK**
Prime examples:: Fishbone, Living Colour, Infectious Grooves

GOTHIC METAL = **HEAVY METAL + DOOM METAL + GOTHIC ROCK**
Prime examples: Type O Negative, Cradle of Filth, Paradise Lost

GROOVE METAL = **THRASH METAL – TEMPO + INTENSE NOISE**
Prime examples: Pantera, Exhorder, Sepultura

INDUSTRIAL METAL = **HEAVY METAL + THRASH METAL + HARDCORE PUNK + ELECTRONIC DANCE**
Prime examples: Nine Inch Nails, KMFDM, Skinny Puppy

MELODIC DEATH METAL = **NEW WAVE OF BRITISH HEAVY METAL + DEATH METAL**
Prime examples: Amon Amarth, Arch Enemy

POWER METAL = **HEAVY METAL + SPEED METAL + HIGH MALE VOCALS + ANTHEMS**
Prime examples: Iron Maiden, Helloween, Gamma Ray

NEOCLASSICAL METAL = **HEAVY METAL + CLASSICAL MUSIC**
Prime examples: Yngwie Malmsteen, Fleshgod Apocalypse, The Human Abstract

NU METAL = **ALTERNATIVE METAL + GROOVE METAL + THRASH METAL + GRUNGE + INDUSTRIAL + FUNK + HIP HOP**
Prime examples: Deftones, Korn, Slipknot

RAP METAL = **HIP HOP + HEAVY METAL + FUNK METAL + CUSSING**
Prime examples: Anthrax, Body Count, Rage Against the Machine

SPEED METAL = **NEW WAVE OF BRITISH HEAVY METAL + HARDCORE PUNK**
Prime examples: Iron Maiden, Motörhead, Sex Machineguns

THRASH METAL = **NEW WAVE OF BRITISH HEAVY METAL + PUNK + HARDCORE + SPEED METAL**
Prime examples: Metallica, Anthrax, Suicidal Tendencies

UNBLACK METAL = **HEAVY METAL + CHRISTIANITY**
Prime examples: Horde, Antestor, Crimson Moonlight

Note: This list represents just a very small number of the very many, many subgenres of metal. Other unexpected offshoots include, but are not limited to: Viking Metal, Blackened Death Metal, Sludge Metal, Medieval Metal, Goregrind, Stoner Metal, and, of course, Pirate Metal.

ROCK KNOWLEDGE

Tragedy struck when Def Leppard drummer Rick Allen lost control of his Corvette and hit a wall on New Year's Eve 1984, losing his arm in the process. However, some good news: a policeman and nurse who attended the accident met for the first time and later married. So that's something.

In this series, we have chosen some of our favourite performers; the artists who embody the Marshall spirit. These are some of the true pioneers of rock – the Legends of Loud.

JOSH HOMME
Axe-weilding Excalibur

If The Devil himself made frontmen, chances are he'd look like Josh Homme. Big, brawny, reassuringly tattooed, and with a dangerous arsenal of dark riffs, no man in music today embodies the very essence of rock more than the Queens of the Stone Age founder. "I'm not a tough guy," claims Homme, "but I am six-foot-five, and I don't like to look away. It's OK to not be macho. But it's not OK to be a pussy."

To prove his point, Homme only plays in tough-sounding bands: Kyuss, Them Crooked Vultures, the Eagles of Death Metal… even Queens of the Stone Age sounds confusingly dangerous. And to prove that he doesn't like to look away, witness Queens' appearance at Glastonbury in 2011. On that year's final Sunday night, when Beyoncé was booked to close proceedings on the Pyramid Stage, the organizers needed someone game or foolish enough to play The Other Stage at the same time. Homme put his hand up. "We found out no one wanted to play against Beyoncé. They asked us, and I was like 'OK, hell yeah'." Unruffled by Queen B, Homme made his intentions clear: "I wanna play so loud that Beyoncé can feel it in her f*cking bones." And he did.

Clearly, then, this is a man with exemplary rock credentials. But don't take our word for it. Consider the evidence of Jesse Hughes, Homme's fellow Eagle of Death Metal. "I'm not calling the man God, but he is carved out of stone by God," he says. "He's a six-foot, five-inch living Excalibur." Amen to that.

SCHOOLS OF ROCK

Twelve rock stars whose brains are possibly bigger than yours...

The Doors' Jim Morrison received an undergraduate degree in film from UCLA.

Weezer's Rivers Cuomo received a bachelor's degree in English from Harvard University.

Art Garfunkel has a master's degree in mathematics from Columbia University.

Rage Against The Machine's Tom Morello graduated from Harvard University with a bachelor's degree in social studies.

Bad Religion's Greg Graffin received a master's degree in geology from UCLA and a PhD in zoology from Cornell University.

Before founding 70s soft rockers **Boston, Tom Scholz** received a bachelor's degree and master's degree in mechanical engineering from the Massachusetts Institute of Technology.

Queen's Brian May received a PhD degree in astrophysics from Imperial College, London.

The Offspring's Dexter Holland has a bachelor's degree in biology and a masters degree in molecular biology from the University of Southern California.

Milo Aukerman of Californian punk rockers **The Descendents** has a doctorate in biochemistry from the University of Wisconsin.

NOFX's Fat Mike has a bachelor's degree in social science and a minor in human sexuality from San Francisco State University.

Post **Guns N'Roses, Duff McKagan** achieved a bachelor's degree in business from Seattle University.

Radiohead's Thom Yorke earned his bachelors degree in fine art and English from the University of Exeter. However, in a band full of brains, he's usurped, academically, by Colin Greenwood, who has a degree in English from Cambridge University.

ROCK KNOWLEDGE

Although Elvis Presley recorded more than 600 songs in his career, he didn't write a single one of them. And while we're at it, The King's hair wasn't black, either, but sandy brown.

AGEING ROCKERS

★★

How far back do the world's greatest rock festivals go?
Approximately this far...

FESTIVAL	★	LOCATION	★	BEGAN
Reading Festival	★	Reading, UK	★	1961
The Isle of Wight, Festival	★	Isle of Wight,UK	★	1968
Glastonbury	★	Somerset, UK	★	1970
Pinkpop, Landgraaf	★	Holland	★	1970
Roskilde Festival	★	Roskilde, Denmark	★	1971
Rock Werchter	★	Werchter, Belgium	★	1974
Rock am Ring	★	Mendig, Germany	★	1985
Pukkelpop	★	Kiewit-Hasselt, Belgium	★	1985
Rock in Rio	★	Rio de Janeiro, Brazil; also other locations	★	1985
Lollapalooza	★	US and various locations worldwide	★	1991
Big Day Out	★	Australia and New Zealand (various locations)	★	1992

ACTORS WHO ROCK!

JACK BLACK TENACIOUS D
Offering his acerbic wit to such films as *High Fidelity* and *School of Rock*, Black branched out into rock as half of comedy band Tenacious D, providing vocals and guitar on three albums.

JOHNNY DEPP P
The *Pirates of the Caribbean* star spent a short time playing guitar in P, the side project band of Butthole Surfers singer Gibby Haynes. Depp is now active in Hollywood Vampires.

RYAN GOSLING DEAD MAN'S BONES
The handsome, if usually mute, actor is one-half of this rock duo, formed in 2008 and with one album to its name. Gosling calls himself Baby Goose and provides vocals, guitar, and piano.

JARED LETO THIRTY SECONDS TO MARS
When not helping himself to an Oscar for his role in *Dallas Buyers Club*, Leto famously fronts Thirty Seconds to Mars. Is he an actor or is he a rock star? Depends what day of the week it is.

JULIETTE LEWIS JULIETTE AND THE LICKS
A feisty actress in such flicks as *Natural Born Killers* and *Cape Fear*, Lewis transformed into the feisty front woman of this indie rock band. Now solo, she has four albums to her credit.

KEANU REEVES DOGSTAR
The star of *Point Break* and *The Matrix* trilogy played bass and provided backing vocals in Dogstar. Though critically dismissed, the group opened for Bon Jovi and gave Weezer its first gig.

ROCKERS WHO ACT!

DAVID BOWIE

In a career spent shape-shifting, of course Bowie branched out into films. His finest turn came as Jareth in *Labyrinth*, playing a goblin king who could transform into a barn owl. As you do.

FLEA

The bass-slapping Chili Pepper boasts a lengthy acting CV that includes, most notably, Douglas J. Needles in *Back to the Future* parts II and III.

DAVE GROHL

A regular on TV, Grohl made his big screen debut in *Tenacious D in The Pick of Destiny*, playing Satan, an axe-wielding red-skinned badass with the teeth of Dracula and the horns of a ram.

COURTNEY LOVE

In an act of art mirroring life, Love played stripper Althea Leasure in *The People vs Larry Flynt*. And she played it so convincingly, it earned her a Golden Globe nomination.

HENRY ROLLINS

On a long-getting-longer acting CV, this legendary punk's big break came in the De Niro/Pacino vehicle *Heat*, playing Hugh Benny, a money-launderer's hired muscle.

STEVEN VAN ZANDT

Bruce Springsteen's trusted guitarist in the E Street Band played one of Tony Soprano's most trusted lieutenants in *The Sopranos*. Just when he thought he was out – and so on and so forth.

THE ICONIC AXE ALMANAC

A brief visual history of rock's greatest guitars.

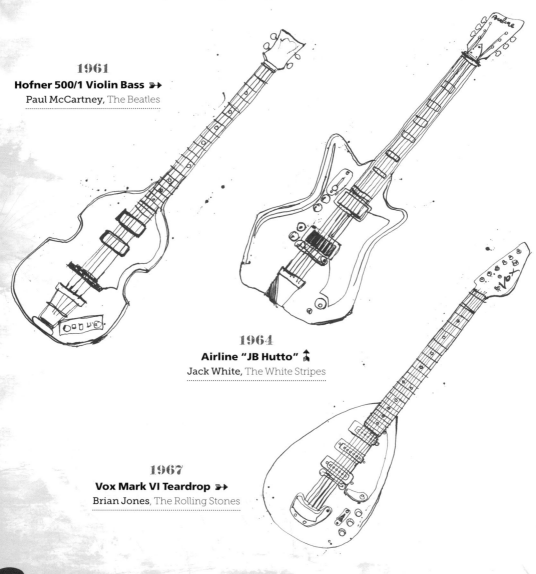

1961
Hofner 500/1 Violin Bass ⮞⮕
Paul McCartney, The Beatles

1964
Airline "JB Hutto" ⬆
Jack White, The White Stripes

1967
Vox Mark VI Teardrop ⮞⮕
Brian Jones, The Rolling Stones

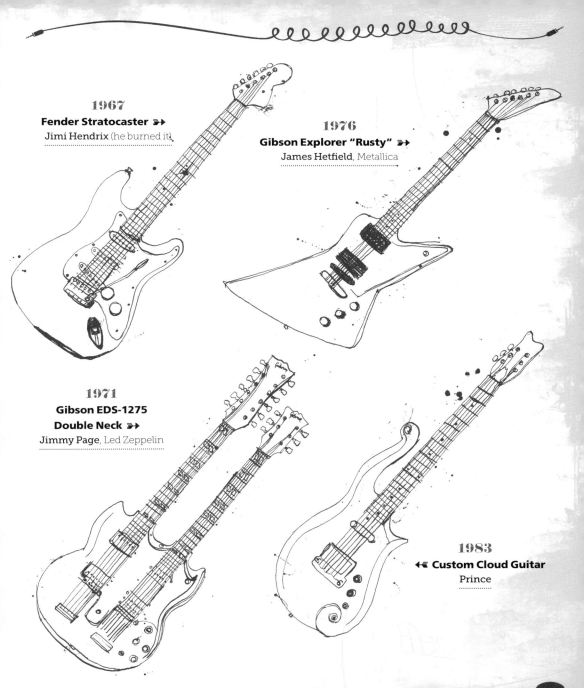

1967
Fender Stratocaster ⇒→
Jimi Hendrix (he burned it)

1976
Gibson Explorer "Rusty" ⇒→
James Hetfield, Metallica

1971
Gibson EDS-1275
Double Neck ⇒→
Jimmy Page, Led Zeppelin

1983
←⇐ **Custom Cloud Guitar**
Prince

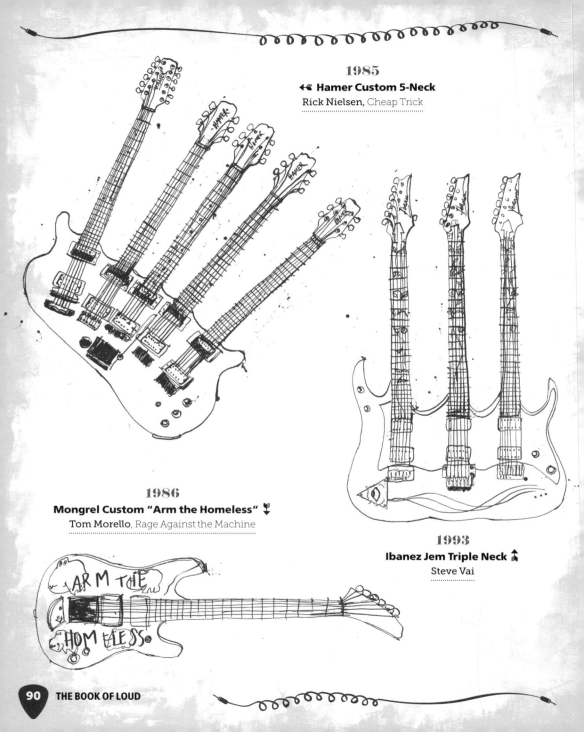

1985
◄◄ Hamer Custom 5-Neck
Rick Nielsen, *Cheap Trick*

1986
Mongrel Custom "Arm the Homeless" ⚑
Tom Morello, *Rage Against the Machine*

1993
Ibanez Jem Triple Neck ⚑
Steve Vai

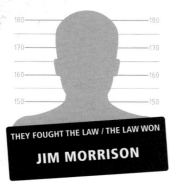

THEY FOUGHT THE LAW / THE LAW WON

JIM MORRISON

No stranger to provocative posturing, the self-proclaimed Lizard King found himself banged up for drunkenly waving his little lizard at an audience of 10,000 at Miami's Dinner Key Auditorium (now the Coconut Grove Convention Center) in 1969. Though no one could prove if Morrison did indeed flash his lizard, the public outcry resulted in the Florida State Attorney's office issuing a warrant for his arrest. Sentenced to six months in jail for indecent exposure and "open profanity", Morrison died in Paris while his appeal was pending. He was pardoned, posthumously, in 2010.

THE MOST EXPENSIVE AXE EVER SOLD AT AUCTION

$2.7 MILLION

Auctioned to raise funds for the survivors of the 2004 Indian Ocean earthquake and tsunami, the Reach Out to Asia Fender Stratocaster sold for a cool $2.7 million (£1.9 million) at Sotheby's, making it the current record-holder for the most expensive axe sold at auction. What made this model unique were the signatures: Eric Clapton, Mick Jagger, Keith Richards, Brian May, Jimmy Page, David Gilmour, Jeff Beck, Pete Townshend, Mark Knopfler, Ray Davis, Liam Gallagher, Ronnie Wood, Tony Iommi, Angus and Malcolm Young, Paul McCartney, Sting, Ritchie Blackmore, Def Leppard, and Bryan Adams all scrawled their names across its white body.

FIVE OTHER VERY COSTLY AXES

JOHN LENNON'S 1962 Gibson J-160E acoustic-electric
$2.41 million (£1.7 million) Julien's Auctions, 2015

BOB DYLAN'S "Newport Folk Festival" Stratocaster
$965,000 (£672,400) Christie's, 2013

ERIC CLAPTON'S "Blackie" Stratocaster Hybrid
$959,500 (£668,593) Christie's, 2004

JERRY GARCIA'S Doug Irwin "Tiger"
$957,500 (£667,114) Guernsey's, 2002

ERIC CLAPTON'S 1964 Gibson ES-335 TDC
$847,500 (£590,550) Christie's 2004

THE SPOTTER'S GUIDE :
THE INDIE KID

Here, learn how to spot the most alternative dude in town, the indie kid.

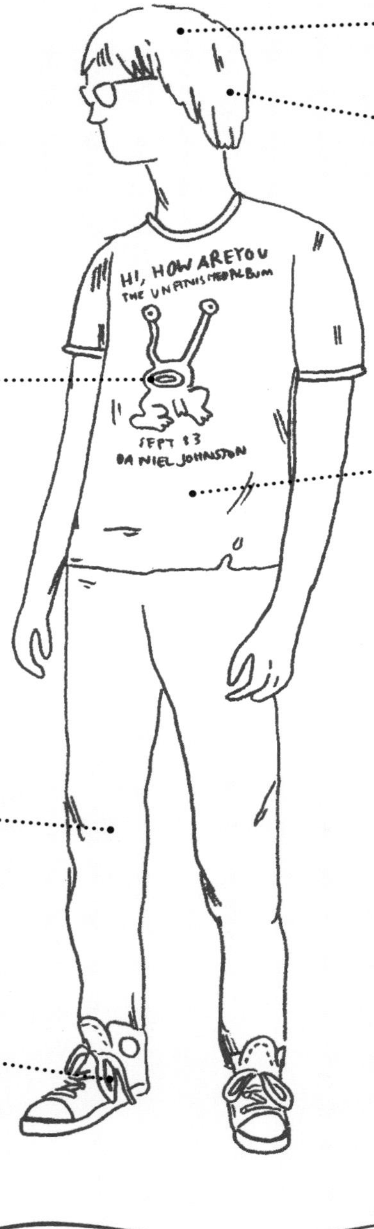

T-shirt bears the legend of an obscure band or a non-brand T in plain, single-tone colour. Either way, it will be frayed, well-worn, and a stranger to soap and water.

Unlike the scene-ster's spray-on jeans, the Indie Kid prefers a looser cut of denim. The jeans have seen better days, but they've also seen more gigs than you.

Footwear means regulation high-tops, but only ever in shades of black or dark blue and tattered to the point of falling apart. Worn until they fall off.

HI, HOW ARE YOU
THE UNFINISHED ALBUM
SEPT #3
DA NIEL JOHNSTON

Inside this head lurk the names of a billion bands you will never have heard of. Some of those bands may not even be real.

Being naturally shy, the Indie Kid (both male and female) hides behind a mop of unruly, unkempt hair. Thick-rimmed spectacles are optional and often entirely unnecessary.

The Indie Kid's skinny frame is less malnourished than yet to be bloated by the passage of time and beer. But it will come. It will.

Listening to:

Bromheads Jacket, *Choro*

Father John Misty, *I Love You, Honeybear*

Public Access TV, *Public Access*

Hinds, *Leave Me Alone*

Bully, *Feels Like*

The Districts, *A Flourish and a Spoil*

Næ'nøcÿbbŒrg VbërrHolökäävsT, *Goodbye, Sol: A Voyage to the End of Spacetime and Back*

Daniel Johnston, *Hi, How Are You*

Orange Juice, *Rip It Up*

DEATH ROCK

The most popular rock songs played at funerals.

British company The Co-operative Funeral Care's list of most popular rock songs played at funerals in the UK is topped by two heavyweights: **Led Zeppelin's** *Stairway to Heaven* and **Queen's** *Who Wants to Live Forever*.

Sadly, the list lumps "Rock" alongside both "Pop" and "Old Favourites", so although Led Zep was the highest-ranked rock entry, it only came in at 14th on the list overall, ahead of Queen (19) but way behind **Frank Sinatra's** *My Way* (1), **Robbie Williams'** *Angels* (2), and **Sarah Brightman and Andrea Bochelli's** *Time to Say Goodbye* (3), but they are clearly not what we know as rock.

As a side note, the top 10 "humorous" tracks played include **Queen's** *Another One Bites the Dust* ranked 3rd, ahead of **Johnny Cash's** *Ring of Fire* (4) and **Meat Loaf's** *Bat Out of Hell* (9).

PETER BUCK (REM)

Boarding a British Airways flight from Seattle to London in April 2001, mild-mannered REM guitarist Buck took a glass of wine, perhaps to steady his pre-flight nerves. Fourteen glasses later he was royally drunk, flipping over a service trolley, covered in yogurt, and assaulting various flight attendants. Arrested on two counts of common assault, plus for being drunk on an aircraft and damaging British Airways crockery, Buck quickly apologized, claiming he had taken a strong sleeping pill and had no knowledge of his performance. He was later cleared.

HOW TO WRITE A GRAMMY AWARD-WINNING ROCK SONG

What we can learn from the 25 winners so far.

RULE 1:
BE A MAN
Of the winners, 76 per cent have been male. The exceptions: Alanis Morissette (1996, 1999) and Tracy Chapman (1997), and male-female duets The White Stripes (2004), Paramore (2015) and Alabama Shakes (2016).

★ ★ ★ ☆ ★ ★ ☆

RULE 2:
WRITE A SONG ABOUT DEATH OR LONELINESS
Death has been the subject of 28 per cent of winning songs – usually the death of a person or people, but on one occasion about the death of a dream. Loneliness is the next most popular subject, covered in 20 per cent of the last 25 winners.

★ ★ ★ ☆ ★ ★ ☆

RULE 3:
MAKE IT ALMOST EXACTLY FOUR MINUTES LONG
The average length of Grammy Award-winning rock song is 4:008 minutes. The shortest track was The Black Keys' Lonely Boy (2013) at 3:14. The longest track: Sting's The Soul Cages (1992) at 5:52.

★ ★ ★ ☆ ★ ★ ☆

RULE 4:
DON'T BE HAPPY
Of the last 25 winners, only one song concerns itself with anything really approaching happiness: Creed's 2001 track With Arms Wide Open, a song about impending fatherhood. That single song represents a pathetic 4 per cent of all 25 winners.

The Winners in Full

YEAR	TRACK	ARTIST	GENDER
1992	*The Soul Cages*	Sting	♂
1993	*Layla*	Eric Clapton	♂
1994	*Runaway Train*	Soul Asylum	♂
1995	*Streets of Philadelphia*	Bruce Springsteen	♂
1996	*You Oughta Know*	Alanis Morissette	♀
1997	*Give Me One Reason*	Tracy Chapman	♀
1998	*One Headlight*	The Wallflowers	♂
1999	*Uninvited*	Alanis Morissette	♀
2000	*Scar Tissue*	Red Hot Chili Peppers	♂
2001	*With Arms Wide Open*	Creed	♂
2002	*Drops of Jupiter (Tell Me)*	Train	♂
2003	*The Rising*	Bruce Springsteen	♂
2004	*Seven Nation Army*	The White Stripes	♂♀
2005	*Vertigo*	U2	♂
2006	*City Of Blinding Lights*	U2	♂
2007	*Dani California*	Red Hot Chili Peppers	♂
2008	*Radio Nowhere*	Bruce Springsteen	♂
2009	*Girls in Their Summer Clothes*	Bruce Springsteen	♂
2010	*Use Somebody*	Kings of Leon	♂
2011	*Angry World*	Neil Young	♂
2012	*Walk*	Foo Fighters	♂
2013	*Lonely Boy*	The Black Keys	♂
2014	*Cut Me Some Slack*	Paul McCartney, Dave Grohl, Krist Novoselic, Pat Smear	♂
2015	*Ain't It Fun*	Paramore	♂♀
2016	*Don't Wanna Fight*	Alabama Shakes	♂♀

In this series, we have chosen some of our favourite performers; the artists who embody the Marshall spirit. These are some of the true pioneers of rock – the Legends of Loud.

KURT COBAIN
Icon of Alienation

From the moment he arrived, Kurt Cobain seemed hell-bent on finding a way back out. *Nevermind* shot Nirvana and Cobain to a level of superstardom he never felt comfortable with. The album took only three and a half weeks to record and was arguably the single most important rock release of the Nineties, a crunching collision of punk nihilism and hard-rock power cut through with Cobain's own vulnerability and alienation.

Buried beneath the frontman's guitar, Dave Grohl's powerhouse drums and Krist Novoselic's dirty, overshadowed bass lay bleak tales of kidnapped girls and of Cobain's days spent sleeping rough, but *Nevermind* was melodic enough to hook the masses – particularly with the album's opener, *Smells Like Teen Spirit*. Following the quiet-loud-quiet dynamic of his own heroes, Cobain later admitted he was ripping off the Pixies and "trying to write the ultimate pop song".

Nevermind knocked King of Pop Michael Jackson off the top of America's Billboard chart and sold in the many millions, but clearly Cobain wasn't happy. He complained that the album had been too polished and went back to basics on its follow-up, the even more uncompromising In Utero. But that didn't bring happiness, either. He took his life in 1994, joining the club of rock stars who died aged 27. "I told him not to join that stupid club," said his mother, but Cobain wasn't listening. He left behind a wife, Courtney Love, and, tragically, a daughter, Frances Bean. The only small consolation was that in *Nevermind*, he also left behind one of rock music's true masterpieces.

COVER STARS

Eleven classic cover versions that might just
be better than the original.

1.
HURT
by Johnny Cash

We tried hard not to opt for the Man in Black's cover of the Nine Inch Nails ode to regret as our top choice, but nothing else comes close. "Hearing it was like someone kissing your girlfriend. It felt invasive," said Trent Reznor, but invasive in a good way. Rick Rubin's pounding piano and the black-and-white video take Hurt to a place Reznor never imagined.

Compare and Contrast: *The Downward Spiral* (1994), *American IV: The Man Comes Around* (2002)

2.
ALL ALONG THE WATCHTOWER
by Jimi Hendrix

Bob Dylan's version wasn't bad. Not classic Dylan, but still impressive in its bluesy, acoustic, harmonica-driven, Dylan-by-numbers kinda way. The Hendrix version was electrifying in more ways than one: a psychedelic, heavy-riffing redux that Jimi entirely made his own.

Compare and Contrast: *John Wesley Harding* (1967), *Electric Ladyland* (1968)

3.
EVERYBODY'S GOT TO LEARN SOMETIME
by Beck

The Korgis' original is pleasant, in a quirky, sounds-older-than-1992 kind of way. The Beck reworking is straighter, quieter, less quirky – and more essential in every way.

Compare and Contrast: *This World's for Everyone* (1992), *Eternal Sunshine of the Spotless Mind* (2004)

4.
I FOUGHT THE LAW
by The Clash

The Bobby Fuller Four's happy-clappy original isn't so far removed from The Clash remake, but the London outfit made it better by adding in a hefty dose of punk bite.

Compare and Contrast: *I Fought the Law* (1966), *The Clash* (1977)

5.
HALLELUJAH
by Jeff Buckley

Of the several million reworkings of Leonard Cohen's sludgy, slower original, Jeff Buckley's soaring and somehow tragic take is by some way the definitive alternative.

Compare and Contrast: *Various Positions* (1984), *Grace* (1994)

6.
LANDSLIDE
by Smashing Pumpkins

It's hard to imagine that Billy Corgan's distinct vocal could improve on the velvet vocals of Stevie Nicks, but here's the evidence that it does. One of the Pumpkins' finest tracks.

Compare and Contrast: *Fleetwood Mac* (1975), *Pisces Iscariot* (1994)

7.
THE MAN WHO SOLD THE WORLD
by Nirvana

The Thin White Duke's original came early on in his career and lacks the focus and finesse given it by Kurt and co. during their MTV Unplugged session.

Compare and Contrast: *The Man Who Sold the World* (1970), *MTV Unplugged in New York* (1994)

8.
LOVE MACHINE
by Arctic Monkeys

The classic Girls Aloud anthem given a dirty karaoke makeover by the Monkeys, and sung, it seems, by a stereotyped northern "turn". Luckily, it's much better than that sounds.

Compare and Contrast: *What Will the Neighbours Say?* (2004), *BBC Radio 1's Live Lounge* (2011)

9.
IMMIGRANT SONG
by Trent Reznor and Atticus Ross

The Led Zep original was a relentless, pounding romp towards Valhalla. The redux followed the same road, but with a techno edge and Karen O's alien vocals. Maybe not better, just different.

Compare and Contrast: *Led Zeppelin III* (1970), *The Girl with the Dragon Tattoo* (2012)

10.
EASY
by Faith No More

In truth, the only real change from the Commodores' original is one filthy Mike Patton "eeugh" towards the end, but that's still enough to elevate an epic to an even higher realm.

Compare and Contrast: *Commodores* (1977), *Angel Dust* (1992)

11.
WONDERWALL
by Ryan Adams

A brave move, this, even to attempt to improve on a beloved original, yet Adams's gently picked acoustic guitar and spooky atmospherics take the Oasis standard in a whole new, more vulnerable direction.

Compare and Contrast: *(What's the Story) Morning Glory* (1995), *Love is Hell* (2004)

ANATOMY OF... A MARSHALL AMP*

The essential rocker kit...

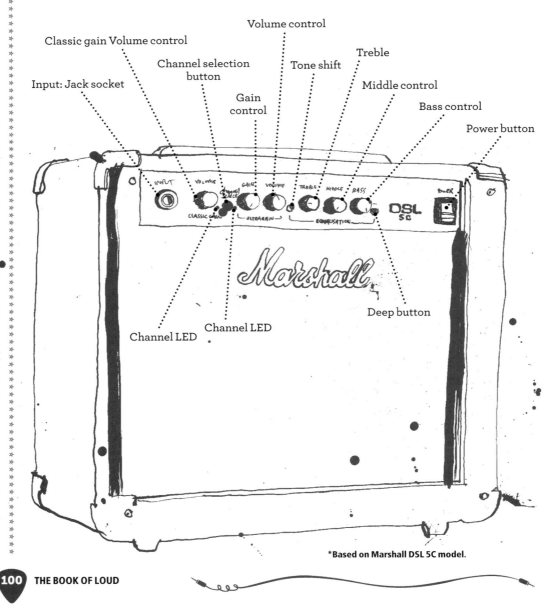

Input: Jack socket

Classic gain Volume control

Channel selection button

Gain control

Volume control

Tone shift

Treble

Middle control

Bass control

Power button

Channel LED

Channel LED

Deep button

*Based on Marshall DSL 5C model.

INPUT
Jack socket for guitar cable. Plug in to make some noise.

CLASSIC GAIN
Classic gain takes you from a shimmering, harmonic-enhanced clean to a 1959-style crunch when the gain control is cranked.

VOLUME CONTROL Controls volume for a nice clean sound.

CHANNEL LED LED lights up to confirm classic gain has been selected.

CHANNEL SELECTION BUTTON Selects ultra gain when pushed in, classic gain when out.

ULTRA GAIN
The ultra gain option takes you into the world of modern high gain and then some.

CHANNEL LED lights red when ultra gain is selected.

GAIN CONTROL increases and decreases distortion levels in your sound.

VOLUME CONTROL controls volume; may or may not hit 11.

EQUALIZATION
TONE SHIFT press to reconfigure and shape the tone – ideal for metal.

TREBLE Changes high frequencies of your axe; turn clockwise for a brighter tone.

MIDDLE CONTROL Tune up to make your axe sound "fatter," down for a sharper "scooped" tone.

BASS CONTROL Determines the amount of bottom-end, low frequencies in your tone.

DEEP BUTTON Press here to add a bass boost to your sound.

POWER BUTTON
On/Off Switch. Let there be light.

ROCK ★ KNOWLEDGE

Despite clearly being Slash from Guns N' Roses, Slash checks into hotels under the name I. P. Freely. This is a common tactic among easily amused rock stars: Kasabian checks in as WWE wrestlers, including Hulk Hogan and Ric Flair, while Ozzy Osbourne prefers the classic Harry Bollocks.

The first CD pressed in the United States was, fittingly, Bruce Springsteen's 1984 album *Born in the USA*. It wasn't the first commercially available CD, though; that was Billy Joel's *52nd Street*, made available to the technological pioneers in Japan in 1982.

The first song used to develop the mp3 was *Tom's Diner* by Suzanne Vega – the supposed "Mother of mp3". Pioneer Karlheinz Brandenburg used the song in testing, playing it thousands of times to fine-tune the compression algorithms used in his new music format.

Nirvana's *Smells Like Teen Spirit* was inspired by a brand of Japanese deodorant, marketed at girls. The line "Kurt smells like Teen Spirit" was daubed on a wall by a friend of Cobain's, though he was said to have no knowledge of the brand when he named the track.

The Muppet Show's manic drummer Animal is thought to have been inspired by either manic Fleetwood Mac drummer Mick Fleetwood, or manic Keith Moon of The Who, depending on which you believe.

THE SPOTTER'S GUIDE :
THE PUNK

Here, learn how to spot the ultimate
seventies rebel, the punk.

Face clean-shaven. Facial hair is not
punk and serves only to detract from the
owner's piercings and skull tattoos.

Sleeveless T-shirt, possibly
bearing obscure band allegiance
and preferably bearing some form
of profanity.

Studded belt, more for show than for
keeping the owner's trousers aligned.

Trousers are denim or tartan, despite
the fact that, more than likely, the owner
is not Scottish. Either way, these will be
ripped and in need of a hot wash.

**Big, black, and bothersome "bovver
boots"** (British slang for skinhead
footwear). Cherry-red also permitted, and
the more eyeholes on show, the better.

Mohawk, starched into dangerous points, the colour chosen at the owner's discretion.

Leather jacket, preferably sleeveless, preferably studded, safety-pinned, and adorned with band patches or painted slogans such as "GBH", "DESTROY", or "BASTARD".

Chain hanging loose from trousers. Traditionally to be used as a weapon in British seaside towns upon the arrival of The Rockers, now it's merely an adornment.

Listening to:

The Clash, *London Calling*

Sex Pistols, *Never Mind the Bollocks ..*

Black Flag, *Damaged*

Ramones, *Rocket to Russia*

Misfits, *Walk Among Us*

Dead Kennedys, *Fresh Fruit for Rotting Vegetables*

NOFX, *Liberal Animation*

Green Day, *Dookie*

Fall Out Boy, *Take This to Your Grave*

My Chemical Romance, *The Black Parade*

TAKE A BITE

Rock's fattest, finest guitar riffs – air axes and imaginary wah-wahs at the ready.

(I Can't Get No) Satisfaction
– Rolling Stones (1965)

Voodoo Child (Slight Return)
– The Jimi Hendrix Experience (1968)

Whole Lotta Love
– Led Zeppelin (1969)

I Wanna Be Your Dog
– The Stooges (1969)

Back in Black
–AC/DC (1980)

Sweet Child O' Mine
– Guns N' Roses (1987)

Smells Like Teen Spirit
– Nirvana (1991)

Enter Sandman
– Metallica (1991)

Plug in Baby
– Muse (2001)

No One Knows
– Queens of the Stone Age (2002)

Seven Nation Army
–The White Stripes (2003)

ELEVEN KARAOKE KILLERS

Where rock karaoke is concerned, these tracks should be approached with caution.

1.
SWEET CHILD O' MINE by Guns N' Roses

Axl Rose always had enough metal menace to get away with his high-pitched vocals on this GN'R standard. You are not Axl and so may struggle – we give you precisely one minute and 16 seconds before you're booed off stage.

2.
SABOTAGE by Beastie Boys

In its glorious entirety it's only 2:58 minutes long, but you don't have the breath to whine for that long. Plus, you don't actually know the words. The end for you will come at 1:52, as the Beasties roar "Waaaaaaaaaaaaaarrrrrr!" You'll have lost the battle – and indeed the war.

3.
CHOP SUEY! by System of a Down

It's alt-metal rap, sung by a man with lungs the size of Armenia. Have a crack, by all means, but you'll likely be bent double and wheezing like a mule before the first minute is out, and dead before it ends.

4.
MONKEY WRENCH by Foo Fighters

At two and a half minutes in, Dave Grohl begins a slow, rising scream that sounds impressively intense when performed by the Foos. Even with your very best efforts, however, it's going to sound deeply unimpressive on the karaoke machine.

5.
MORE THAN A FEELING by Boston

Mercifully, for all involved, the sobering realization that you do not possess the lungs or range to do this karaoke classic justice will be swift. After just 30 seconds, you will be out of your depth and waving a pretend white flag.

6.
IT'S THE END OF THE WORLD AS WE KNOW IT by REM

You'll be fine for the first 10 seconds or so with this one, as you gamely keep pace with Michael Stipe's opening salvo. Thereafter, you won't have a prayer – Stipe hits warp speed and you'll be left spluttering in his dust.

7.
I BELIEVE IN A THING CALLED LOVE by The Darkness

From the same school as AC/DC's You Shook Me All Night Long, here's a song your limited range cannot do justice to. The first of many rising high notes arrives as early as 30 seconds in, at which point you should have already made your exit.

8.

UNDER PRESSURE **by Queen and David Bowie**

The incomparable Freddie Mercury can just about get away with scat-warbling "dee ba dee ba deep, de da dee da dee da" over four long minutes. You? No, you can't.

....

9.

GIRLS GIRLS GIRLS **by Mötley Crüe**

Cock rock can't be that hard, surely? You'd have guessed not, but your starting point for this Crüe classic is a high-pitched falsetto wail, And from there it only climbs higher.

....

10.

HOTEL CALIFORNIA **by The Eagles**

Vocally, there's nothing much to fear here; this is gentle country rock within the range of most mere mortals. However, the fact that it weighs in at a narcolepsy-inducing 6:31 means you shouldn't ever, under any circumstances, even consider it.

....

11.

MORE THAN WORDS **by Extreme**

Just because.

....

SEVEN DAYS OF ROCK

Monday
by Wilco

Tuesday's Gone
by Lynyrd Skynyrd

Wednesday's Song
by John Frusciante

Thursday
by Morphine

Black Friday
by Faith No More

Saturday Superhouse
by Biffy Clyro

Sunday Sun
by Beck

★ ★

In this series, we have chosen some of our favourite performers; the artists who embody the Marshall spirit. These are some of the true pioneers of rock – the Legends of Loud.

JIMI HENDRIX

Psychedelic Voodoochild

Johnny Allen Hendrix lived fast and burned out all too early. But during his short time orbiting our planet, Hendrix did more to redefine rock music than anyone before or since.

Born Johnny but renamed James Marshall Hendrix at the age of four, Jimi picked up his first guitar at 16, an acoustic bought for $5 (about £3.50). A year later he went electric, but the US Army soon got in the way of fame – they made him cut his hair short and shave, and such a regimented lifestyle was entirely at odds with Hendrix. An honourable discharge was granted in 1962 – at which point Jimi Hendrix was reborn.

Part Cherokee, part African-American, drainpipe-thin but with his wild Afro regrown, Hendrix soon became the most visionary guitarist the world would ever see. A left-hander playing a right-handed guitar without restringing it, Hendrix played a blend of psychedelic blues and funk previously unheard, shredding his guitar with his teeth, setting it on fire both figuratively and literally.

"He played just about every style you could think of, and not in a flashy way," said Eric Clapton years later. "He walked off, and my life was never the same again."

Hendrix was epiphanic for all who heard him, but his star burned out too soon. Dead aged just 27, he left behind just three studio albums, all squeezed into the two short years of 1967 and '68, and a legendary performance at Woodstock in 1969. Almost half a century later, everything Jimi Hendrix achieved reverberates through rock music.

SCHOOL OF ROCK

How to... Pull Off an Air Guitar Move

Anyone can play guitar, as Radiohead once sang, so absolutely anyone can play air guitar. That said, to elevate your performance above the rabble, throw in one of rock's signature moves.

THE CHUCK BERRY "DUCK WALK"

Created in 1956, Chuck Berry's classic duck walk looks more fiddly than it actually is. Simply squat on your chosen leg, then hop along on it as your other leg swings back and forth. For Chuck, it was made more complicated by having to keep playing his guitar, but that's not something you need to worry about tonight.

WORKS BEST ON: *Johnny B. Goode*

THE PETE TOWNSHEND "WINDMILL"

With feet firmly planted wide for a strong foundation, take your chosen arm backwards and strum down on the strings in time with the track. For drama, rev the arm up with every rotation and repeat until the music or your energy run out. Townshend famously caught and mangled his hand in the whammy bar once, but your guitar is entirely imaginary and should present no such issues.

WORKS BEST ON: *Won't Get Fooled Again*

THE JIMI HENDRIX "TEETH SOLO"

One of several tricks employed by perhaps the greatest guitar god on Planet Rock, Hendrix regularly played the damn thing between his legs, behind his back, and – as we're suggesting here – using his pearly whites. So, simply pull your imaginary axe from its regular position up to teeth level, then pluck away in time with Jimi's sweet kisses. Pause only to kiss the sky (or that guy, if you've misheard the lyric) then get back to it.

WORKS BEST ON: *Angel*

KILLER AIR AXE TRACKS

The Who – *Baba O'Riley*

Boston – *More Than a Feeling*

Lynyrd Skynyrd – *Free Bird*

AC/DC – *You Shook Me All Night Long*

Weezer – *Hash Pipe*

Foo Fighters – *Monkey Wrench*

Black Sabbath – *War Pigs*

The Hives – *Hate To Say I Told You So*

Radiohead – *Paranoid Android*

Cream – *Sunshine Of Your Love*

The White Stripes – *Seven Nation Army*

Queens Of The Stone Age – *No One Knows*

Motörhead – *Ace Of Spades*

Muse – *Plug In Baby*

Jimi Hendrix – *Purple Haze*

AC/DC – *Thunderstruck*

Guns N'Roses – *Sweet Child O' Mine*

Metallica – *Enter Sandman*

10 A.M. Automatic – *The Black Keys*

AT THE DRIVE-IN

* *

Presenting what may well be rock music's 11 greatest movies.

1.
THIS IS SPINAL TAP (1984)

The mockumentary – rockumentary, if you will – that defines the entire genre. Tap is a creation that despite its advancing years gets funnier with every viewing. Eddie van Halen wondered why all his friends were in hysterics when he first saw it, as he'd lived every scene in real life. And it has the added bonus of Tap guitarist Nigel Tufnel turning his Marshall amps all the way to 11.

2.
DAZED AND CONFUSED (1993)

Richard Linklater's ode to his late-Seventies school days: bongs, sixers, paddles, and all. Worth it for the soundtrack alone, if not for David Wooderson – and significantly better than alright, alright, alright.

3.
SOME KIND OF MONSTER (2004)

The story of Metallica in meltdown, a band at war with each other, with the creative well-run-dry and with a therapist rubbing his hands. Almost as awkward as it is entertaining, which it is in spades.

4.
ANVIL: THE STORY OF ANVIL (2008)

A struggling rock band chase one final shot at stardom, despite all logic suggesting stardom long since left town. Repeated humiliation duly follows in what is an essential, tragic, uplifting cross between Spinal Tap and The Wrestler.

5.
24 HOUR PARTY PEOPLE (2002)

The retelling of Manchester's pioneering indie music scene, charting the rise and fall of the legendary Factory Records. A comical, calamitous tale, soundtracked by some of the era's – and rock's – greatest tracks.

6.
DIG! (2005)

Dig! followed the diverging paths of indie-rock friends Anton Newcombe of the Brian Jonestown Massacre and Courtney Taylor of The Dandy Warhols over seven years. That you know which of them made it and which of them didn't doesn't detract from a painful tale.

7.
CONTROL (2007)

Shot in black-and-white and as beautiful as it is entertaining, celebrated photographer Anton Corbijn's Control retells the demise of Joy Division and their tragic frontman, Ian Curtis. You know how it ends, but that hardly matters.

8.

ALMOST FAMOUS (2000)

Cameron Crowe's slightly fictionalized tale of his time as a teenage rock journalist, writing features as a wide-eyed Rolling Stone magazine intern in the 1970s. Benefits massively from a killer soundtrack, which introduced Elton John's epic Tiny Dancer to a whole new generation.

....

9.

HIGH FIDELITY (2000)

Nick Hornby's tale of music (and list) obsession at the expense of human relationships, relocated from London to Chicago and with Bruce Springsteen playing an unexpected walk-on part. Well, not unexpected now.

....

10.

SCHOOL OF ROCK (2003)

In which the divisive Jack Black plays Dewey Finn, a substitute teacher just kicked out of a rock band. When he turns up at a stuffy elementary private school, the rest of the film writes itself, but writes it well.

....

11.

THE DOORS (1991)

So bad it was excellent. Val Kilmer as The Lizard King, Oliver Stone on directorial duty, this was panned at the time, but as the very sharp spike in sales illustrated, The Doors turned a whole new generation on to The Doors.

....

ROCK KNOWLEDGE

On trusted film ranking website IMDb, the only title ranked out of 11 instead of the standard 10 is, of course, Spinal Tap.

THE BEGINNING IS THE END

The shortest record in the history of rock.

Officially, according to the Guinness World Records, the shortest song ever recorded is *You Suffer* by Napalm Death, which clocks in at just **1.316 seconds** long and contains just two lines: "You suffer. But why?"

QUICK RELEASE

Ten other tracks that won't keep you long.

SONG TITLE		BAND		LENGTH
Air Conditioners In the Woods	★	Grandaddy	★	0:05
26 Second Song	★	My Morning Jacket	★	0:27
Cycle	★	Beck	★	0:40
Murder the Government	★	NOFX	★	0:46
Wasted	★	Black Flag	★	0:51
Lukin	★	Pearl Jam	★	1:02
Come On!	★	The Hives	★	1:09
Fragile	★	The Lemonheads	★	1:20
Big Man with a Gun	★	NIN	★	1:36
Fell in Love with a Girl	★	The White Stripes	★	1:50

THEY FOUGHT THE LAW / THE LAW WON

KEITH MOON

In a short but spectacular lifetime spent pounding drums and wreaking havoc, The Who's insane sticks-man was collared while celebrating his birthday at a Holiday Inn at Flint, Michigan, in 1967. What started out as a food fight soon escalated into a full-scale riot, with rooms trashed, toilets blown up with dynamite, pianos destroyed, and a Lincoln Continental rolled into the hotel swimming pool with a naked, heavily intoxicated Moon behind the wheel. Arrested but released, The Who were hit with a $24,000 bill for damages and banned from the hotel.

DEAR MTV...

In 1996, the magnificent Dark Lord Nick Cave received a nomination for MTV's Best Male Artist. Unexpectedly, to some at least, Cave decided to remove his hat from the ring, writing a letter addressed "to all those at MTV". In capitals, it read:

TO ALL THOSE AT MTV,

I WOULD LIKE TO START BY THANKING YOU ALL FOR THE SUPPORT YOU HAVE GIVEN ME OVER RECENT YEARS, AND I AM BOTH GRATEFUL AND FLATTERED BY THE NOMINATIONS THAT I HAVE RECEIVED FOR BEST MALE ARTIST. THE AIRPLAY GIVEN TO BOTH THE KYLIE MINOGUE AND P. J. HARVEY DUETS FROM MY LATEST ALBUM MURDER BALLADS HAS NOT GONE UNNOTICED AND HAS BEEN GREATLY APPRECIATED. SO AGAIN, MY SINCERE THANKS.

HAVING SAID THAT, I FEEL THAT IT'S NECESSARY FOR ME TO REQUEST THAT MY NOMINATION FOR BEST MALE ARTIST BE WITHDRAWN AND FURTHERMORE ANY AWARDS OR NOMINATIONS FOR SUCH AWARDS THAT MAY ARISE IN LATER YEARS BE PRESENTED TO THOSE WHO FEEL MORE COMFORTABLE WITH THE COMPETITIVE NATURE OF THESE AWARD CEREMONIES. I MYSELF, DO NOT. I HAVE ALWAYS BEEN OF THE OPINION THAT MY MUSIC IS UNIQUE AND INDIVIDUAL AND EXISTS BEYOND THE REALMS INHABITED BY THOSE WHO WOULD REDUCE THINGS TO MERE MEASURING. I AM IN COMPETITION WITH NO ONE.

MY RELATIONSHIP WITH MY MUSE IS A DELICATE ONE AT THE BEST OF TIMES AND I FEEL THAT IT IS MY DUTY TO PROTECT HER FROM INFLUENCES THAT MAY OFFEND HER FRAGILE NATURE.

SHE COMES TO ME WITH THE GIFT OF SONG AND IN RETURN I TREAT HER WITH THE RESPECT I FEEL SHE DESERVES – IN THIS CASE THIS MEANS NOT SUBJECTING HER TO THE INDIGNITIES OF JUDGEMENT AND COMPETITION. MY MUSE IS NOT A HORSE AND I AM IN NO HORSE RACE AND IF INDEED SHE WAS, STILL I WOULD NOT HARNESS HER TO THIS TUMBRIL – THIS BLOODY CART OF SEVERED HEADS AND GLITTERING PRIZES. MY MUSE MAY SPOOK! MAY BOLT! MAY ABANDON ME COMPLETELY!

SO ONCE AGAIN, TO THE PEOPLE AT MTV, I APPRECIATE THE ZEAL AND ENERGY THAT WAS PUT BEHIND MY LAST RECORD, I TRULY DO AND SAY THANK YOU AND AGAIN I SAY THANK YOU BUT NO... NO, THANK YOU.

YOURS SINCERELY,
NICK CAVE
21 OCTOBER 1996

THE STYLE OF ROCK: *THE MAN BEHIND THE MASK*

A brief history of masked rockers.

PAPA EMERITUS ♟

The lead singer of Swedish metal band Ghost, Papa Emeritus is a Satanic priest, flanked by five Nameless (and anonymous) Ghouls, each representing one of the five elements of fire, water, wind, earth, and ether. The man behind the make-up may change – we're now up to Papa Emeritus III – but the colours remain the same: black and white and shaped like a skull.

BUCKETHEAD ♟

Plain white mask, inspired by Michael Myers in Halloween 4. Regulation KFC "hat" inspired by the Colonel's family chicken bucket. The idea came while prolific shredder Brian Carroll was eating KFC. "I put the mask on and then the bucket on my head. I went to the mirror. I just said, 'Buckethead. That's Buckethead right there.' And it was."

KISS ♟

Take four faces, add a thick smudge of black grease and zinc oxide cream and lo: you now have The Starchild, The Demon, The Spaceman, and The Catman, collectively known as cartoon metal legends Kiss. Some may argue that the members of Kiss are too old for make-up. Others point out that because they're so old, they need that make-up more than ever.

MUMMIES ⬇

The self-proclaimed "Kings of Budget Rock" always shunned the trappings of modern rock – recording on ancient, damaged equipment, releasing only on vinyl for many years and ignoring the rise of social media as a way of building their, erm, brand. They also dressed in head to toe in bandages, leaving just enough room to make noise. Because – well, just because.

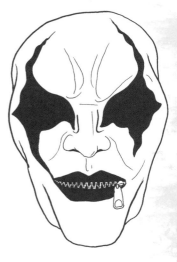

GWAR ⬆

A frequently rotating line-up of artists drawn from the collective known as Slave Pit Inc, GWAR go about their business dressed from top to toe as hellish interplanetary warriors with a nasty glint in their eye. That business of theirs is shock-rock heavy metal – a brand heavy on themes of sadistic sex and ultra-violence and featuring such releases as Scumdogs of the Universe and This Toilet Earth. Approach with caution.

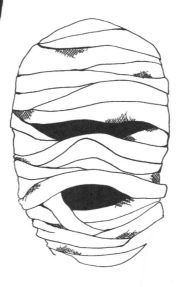

SLIPKNOT ⬆

The members of the Des Moines nu-metal collective hide their identities behind masks designed to scare small children. "It's our way of becoming more intimate with the music," claimed Corey Taylor in 2002, "a way for us to become unconscious of who we are and what we do outside of music." The masks are as changeable as the members in the band and range in style from grim and gruesome to gruesome and grim.

SDRAWKCABTINIPS

Six songs allegedly containing reverse messages.

Back when bands released all their music on vinyl, some were said to engage in the act of "back-masking": a sly trick in which songs played backwards could be found to contain hidden and sometimes subliminal messages. Subversive intent or an unfortunate accident? Judge for yourself on the following tracks.

On
STAIRWAY TO HEAVEN
by Led Zeppelin

During the "If there's a bustle in your hedgerow, don't be alarmed now" passage, the phrase "Here's to my sweet Satan" can supposedly be heard.

On
ULTRAMEGA OK
by Soundgarden

In what was considered to be a response to the number of supposedly satanic messages on records, the Seattle grungers inserted "I love you, Santa baby" onto their 1988 album.

On
MICHAEL
by Franz Ferdinand

Easily audible, the art-indie rockers buried the message "She worries about you, call your mother" on their 2004 track.

On
REVOLUTION 9
by The Beatles

The song is said to contain the instruction "Turn me on, dead man", giving weight to the conspiracy theory that Paul McCartney has actually been dead since 1966.

On
MOTORCADE OF GENEROSITY
by Cake

A clear and helpful reminder on the California alt-rockers 1994 album. As the noise subsides, "Don't forget to breathe in" is clearly audible.

On
REVELATION #9
by Marilyn Manson

A man with a supposed penchant for backtracking, "If anyone's playing this backwards: How you doing? How you doing?" can be heard, before he begins to make lewd remarks about your mother.

IT'S A FAMILY AFFAIR

A brief overview of siblings who rock.

The Butler Brothers
33% of Arcade Fire
Win (vocals, guitar) and Will (bass)

The Robinson Brothers
33% of The Black Crowes
Chris (singer) and Rich (guitar)

The Greenwood Brothers
40% of Radiohead
Jonny (guitar) and Colin (bass)

The Asheton Brothers
40% of The Stooges
Scott (drums) and Ron (guitar)

The Hawkins Brothers
50% of The Darkness
Justin (vocals, guitar) and Dan (guitar)

The Gallagher Brothers
40% of Oasis
Noel (guitar, vocals) and Liam (vocals, tambourine)

The Reid Brothers
40% of The Jesus and Mary Chain
Jim (vocals, guitar) and William (guitar, vocals)

The Deal Sisters
50% of The Breeders
Kim (vocals, guitar) and Kelley (guitar)

The Davies Brothers
50% of The Kinks
Ray (vocals, guitar) and Dave (guitar)

The DeLeo Brothers
50% of Stone Temple Pilots
Robert (bass) and Dean (guitar)

The Van Halen Brothers
50% of Van Halen
Eddie (guitar) and Alex (drums) (plus Eddie's son, Wolfgang Van Halen on guitar, which takes the Van Halen Van Halen total to 75%)

The Young Brothers
66% of AC/DC (original lineup)
Angus (lead guitar) and Malcolm (rhythm guitar)

The Followill Brothers
75% of Kings of Leon
Caleb (singer), Nathan (bass) and Jared (drummer) (plus cousin Matthew on guitar)

The Dessner/Devendorf Brothers
80% of The National
Aaron (guitar) and Bryce (guitar) / Scott (bass and Bryan (drums)

The Mael Brothers
100% of Sparks
Ron (Keyboards) and Russell (vocals)

* *

In this series, we have chosen some of our favourite performers; the artists who embody the Marshall spirit. These are some of the true pioneers of rock – the Legends of Loud.

SLASH
The axe man cometh

Question: What connects a stolen hat, David Bowie's clothes and some of the most famous guitar riffs in history?

Answer: Saul "Slash" Hudson, the high-hatted lead guitarist for rock behemoths Guns N' Roses and Velvet Revolver. Slash became a household name after joining GNR in 1985, and was quick to hit the heights of rock royalty with his searing riffs on songs such as *Sweet Child O' Mine* and the sonic explosion of *Welcome to the Jungle*.

Slash – so-called because he was always running around from place to place – grew up in a creative hot house, the offspring of Ola Hudson, who designed costumes for David Bowie, and Anthony Hudson, designer of album covers for the likes of Neil Young and Joni Mitchell. He played a drum in a school production of The Twelve Days of Christmas, aged five, but the skins were never his true calling and drumming's loss was soon to be hard-rock guitar's gain.

Slash dove head-first into the Los Angeles music scene, bouncing around from band to band until Axl Rose and Izzy Stradlin asked him to become a part of Guns N' Roses. After knocking out a few critically acclaimed and publicly adored albums, the band were megastars, intent on living the rock-star life to the fullest with stories of excess, indulgence and riots. But it couldn't last. Fast forward a few years, to 1996, and GNR were no more and Slash went on to form Velvet Revolver.

The last couple of decades have been rife with talk of the original Guns reforming, but the stars had never realigned. Until now. In 2016, Slash broke the news that finally, they were getting the band back together. And the whole merry-go-round began again…

And the hat? Slash claims that he stole it from a clothing store before a show, saying that wearing it gave him the confidence to perform in front of big crowds. And as long as it means he's still performing, who are we to argue?

ROCK'S SIX GREATEST DRUMMERS

Behind every legendary band sits a legendary drummer. Here we present six of the very best.

1.
JOHN BONHAM (Led Zeppelin)

The baddest bad-ass drummer in the history of rock, Bonham was the backbone of Led Zeppelin, bringing speed, intensity, muscle, and a sense of soul like no other before or since. The drummer the very greatest call The Greatest – yet that accolade doesn't even come close.

His finest hour... *Black Dog*

2.
KEITH MOON (The Who)

A man whose legendary rock 'n' roll excess couldn't overshadow his ability as the beating heart of The Who. "Moon the Loon" treated his drum kit like a weapon of mass destruction, bringing a reckless intensity few could match. Rock's original drummer, and arguably its very best.

His finest hour... *Won't Get Fooled Again*

3.
DAVE GROHL (Various)

Providing the muscle for Nirvana, Queens of the Stone Age, Them Crooked Vultures and, on occasion, Nine Inch Nails, Grohl mixes precision with pulverzation to astounding effect. When he's not busy further forward, Grohl is modern-rock's most influential, dependable sticks man.

His finest hour... *A Song for the Dead* (Queens of the Stone Age)

4.
LARS ULRICH (Metallica)

Metallica's sticks man takes an impressive less-is-more approach, always eschewing frills and flash in favour of the basics, delivered hard and fast and with the great Dane's unrelenting energy. Except on the ballads.

His finest hour... *Cyanide*

5.
THOMAS PRIDGEN (Various)

If John Bonham had incorporated a little salsa, funkadelic, and Afrobeat into his Led Zeppelin rhythms, he'd have sounded a lot like The Mars Volta's Pridgen, an eight-armed drumming machine.

His finest hour... *Goliath* (The Mars Volta)

6.
JOSH FREESE (Various)

Edging out such big guns as Charlie Watts, Jane's Addiction's Stephen Perkins, and Animal from the Muppets, Freese graces the list for the breadth of his influence, pounding out the beats for bands as diverse as Devo, Nine Inch Nails, The Vandals, Guns N' Roses, and Weezer. The most celebrated – and thunderous – drummer-for-hire at work today.

His finest hour... *Wish* (Nine Inch Nails, live version – search for it, you won't be disappointed).

ROCK FOR HIRE

Want to hire your favourite rock band for a private gig, a country fair, a corporate gig, or a concert in the park. Well, here's how much you'd need to pay.*

BAND	FEE		BAND	FEE
Aerosmith	**$500,000-$1m**	★	Muse	**$500,000-$1m**
Alice Cooper	$40,000-$74,999	★	NERD	$75,000-$149,999
Andrew W.K.	$15,000-$24,999	★	Nine Inch Nails	$150,000-$299,000
Arcade Fire	**$500,000-$1m**	★	Pixies	$150,000-$299,000
Arctic Monkeys	**$500,000-$1m**	★	Radiohead	$150,000-$299,000
Biffy Clyro	$75,000-$149,999	★	Red Hot Chili Peppers	**$500,000-$1m**
Black Sabbath	$75,000-$149,999	★	Royal Blood	$7,500-$14,999
Cat Power	$75,000-$149,999	★	Ryan Adams	$40,000-$74,999
Coldplay	**$500,000-$1m**	★	Slipknot	$300,000-$499,000
Courtney Love	$25,000-$39,999	★	Smashing Pumpkins	$300,000-$499,000
Dave Grohl (solo)	**$500,000-$1m**	★	Soundgarden	$300,000-$499,000
Death Cab for Cutie	$300,000-$499,000	★	The Cult	$75,000-$149,999
Faith No More	**$500,000-$1m**	★	The Cure	**$500,000-$1m**
Fall Out Boy	$150,000-$299,000	★	The Killers	**$500,000-$1m**
Flaming Lips	$150,000-$299,000	★	The Offspring	$150,000-$299,000
Jack White	**$500,000-$1m**	★	The Shins	$300,000-$499,000
Jane's Addiction	$300,000-$499,000	★	The Strokes	$40,000-$74,999
Kid Rock	**$500,000-$1m**	★	The XX	$40,000-$74,999
Kings of Leon	**$500,000-$1m**	★	Vampire Weekend	$150,000-$299,000
Korn	$150,000-$299,000	★	Weezer	$300,000-$499,000
L7	$7,500-$14,999	★	Wilco	$40,000-$74,999
Limp Bizkit	$300,000-$499,000	★	Yeah Yeah Yeahs	$40,000-$74,999
Linkin Park	**$500,000-$1m**	★	ZZ Top	**$500,000-$1m**

*Fees according to Celebrity Talent International. Figures listed are minimum fees and for U.S. dates only. Figures correct at time of press.

STAIRWAYS TO HEAVEN

Where in the world you can find your favourite deceased rock star…

JIM MORRISON 1943–71
Buried at Père Lachaise Cemetery, Paris, France.

JIMI HENDRIX 1942–70
Buried at Greenview Memorial Cemetery, Renton, Washington.

JOHNNY CASH 1932–2003
Buried at 353 Johnny Cash Parkway, Hendersonville, Tennessee (beside his wife, June Carter).

FREDDIE MERCURY 1946–91
Memorial at Montreux, Lake Geneva, Switzerland (ashes scattered in Lake Geneva, statue overlooking the lake).

KURT COBAIN 1967–94
Memorials at Viretta Park, Seattle, Washington, USA (ashes scattered in Washington's Wishkah River and park bench memorials in Viretta Park).

JOHN BONHAM 1948–80
Buried at St Michael Churchyard, Rushock, Wyre Forest District, Worcestershire, England.

JEFF BUCKLEY 1966–97
Memorial at Memphis Zoo, Memphis, Shelby County, Tennessee, USA (location of ashes unreported but there's a memorial marker located overlooking the Sumatran Tigers at the Memphis Zoo).

KEITH MOON 1946–78
Cremated at Golders Green Crematorium, Golders Green, London, England (ashes scattered in the Gardens of Remembrance).

PHIL LYNOTT 1949–86
Buried at Saint Fintan's Cemetery, Dublin, Ireland.

SID VICIOUS 1957–79
Ashes at King David Memorial Park, Bensalem, Bucks County, Pennsylvania, USA (reportedly scattered on grave of girlfriend, Nancy Spungen).

DAVID BOWIE 1947–2016
Ashes scattered near Woodstock, Ulster County, New York, USA (reportedly scattered in Catskills Mountains, close to the home in which Bowie died).

HILLEL SLOVAK 1962–88
Buried at Mount Sinai Memorial Park, Los Angeles, Los Angeles County, California, USA.

JOHN LENNON 1940–80
Ashes scattered at Strawberry Fields Memorial, Central Park, New York, USA (cremated at Ferncliff Cemetery, New York, location of ashes is unconfirmed).

JANIS JOPLIN 1943–70
Ashes scattered at Stinson Beach, Marin County, California, USA (cremated in LA, ashes scattered in Pacific Ocean and along Stinson Beach, California).

BON SCOTT (AC/DC) 1946–80
Buried at Fremantle Cemetery, Fremantle, Western Australia.

IAN CURTIS 1956–80
Buried at Macclesfield Cemetery, 77 Barton Street, Macclesfield, Cheshire, UK.

IN THE CLUB

The artists and bands who've made it into America's
esteemed Rock and Roll Hall of Fame.

The Rock and Roll Hall of Fame was founded in 1983, created to "recognize the contributions of those who have had a significant impact on the evolution, development, and perpetuation of rock and roll". Three years later it began inducting its first artists, who only become eligible for induction 25 years after the release of their first record. Today, there are way too many inductees to list here, but a selected recap illustrates the acts that have shaped rock music's landscape. They include:

YEAR	ARTIST	YEAR	ARTIST
1986	Chuck Berry * James Brown * Elvis Presley	2001	Aerosmith * Queen
1987	Bo Diddley * Marvin Gaye * Aretha Franklin	2002	Tom Petty and the Heartbreakers
1988	The Beatles * Bob Dylan	2003	AC * DC
1989	The Rolling Stones	2004	ZZ Top
1990	The Who	2005	U2
1991	The Byrds	2006	Black Sabbath * Lynyrd Skynyrd
1992	Johnny Cash * The Jimi Hendrix Experience	2007	R.E.M.
1993	The Doors	2008	The Ventures
1994	The Grateful Dead * John Lennon	2009	Metallica
1995	Led Zeppelin * Neil Young	2010	The Stooges
1996	David Bowie * Pink Floyd	2011	Alice Cooper
1997	Buffalo Springfield	2012	Red Hot Chili Peppers * Guns N' Roses * Beastie Boys
1998	The Eagles * Fleetwood Mac	2013	Public Enemy
1999	Bruce Springsteen	2014	Nirvana
2000	Eric Clapton	2015	Green Day
		2016	Cheap Trick * Chicago * N.W.A.

THE OFFSPRING

✳✳✳

The names famous rock stars saddle their kids with.

SEX OF CHILD	NAME	STAR PARENT(S)
♂	Zuma Nesta Rock	Gavin Rossdale (Zuma is brother to **Kingston James McGregor** and **Apollo Bowie Flynn**)
♀	Frances Bean	Kurt Cobain and Courtney Love
♂	Everly Bear	Anthony Kiedis
♂	Jonas Rocket	Tom DeLonge
♀	Diva Thin Muffin Pigeen	Frank Zappa (Diva is sister to **Dweezil ♂** and **Moon Unit ♀**)
♂	Bronx Mowgli	Pete Wentz
♀	Mirabella Bunny	Bryan Adams
♂	Bingham	Matt Bellamy
♀	Omri	Jonny Greenwood
♀	Blue Angel	The Edge
♂	Dylan Jagger	Tommy Lee and Pamela Anderson
♀	Bandit Lee	Gerard Way

◆◆◆ ◆◆◆ ◆◆◆ ◆◆◆ ◆◆◆ ◆◆◆ ◆◆◆ ◆◆◆ ◆◆◆ ◆◆◆ ◆◆◆ ◆◆◆ ◆◆◆ ◆◆◆ ◆◆◆ ◆◆◆ ◆◆◆ ◆◆◆ ◆◆◆ ◆◆◆

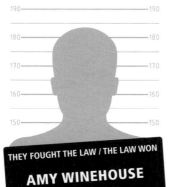

190 — 190
180 — 180
170 — 170
160 — 160
150 — 150

THEY FOUGHT THE LAW / THE LAW WON

AMY WINEHOUSE

A self-destructive taste for illegal substances ensured that Winehouse and London's Camden constabulary were on first-name terms, but in a less-expected twist, the tattooed chanteuse was arrested after attending a performance of Cinderella at the Milton Keynes Theatre in England in 2009. Having loudly heckled the actors throughout the performance, Winehouse was asked to leave, whereupon she attacked a member of staff and was duly charged with a public-order offense and common assault. She received a two-year conditional discharge and paid £85 in costs and £100 in compensation.

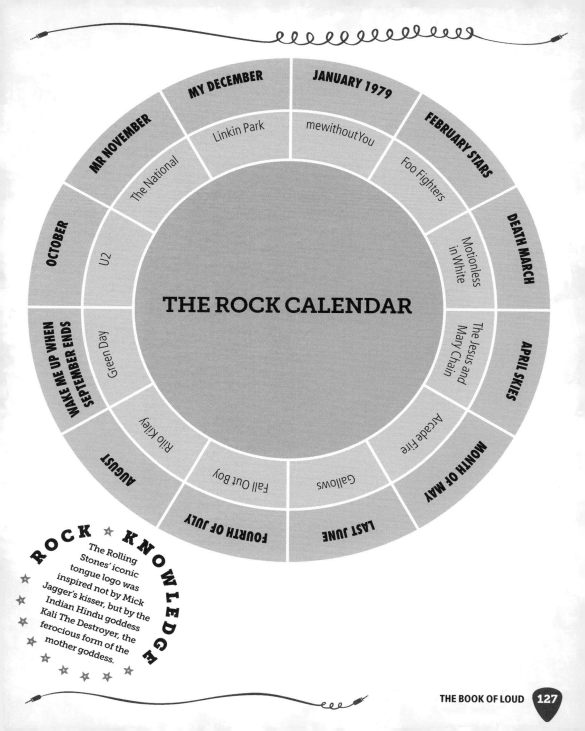

THE ROCK CALENDAR

JANUARY 1979 — mewithoutYou

MY DECEMBER — Linkin Park

MR NOVEMBER — The National

OCTOBER — U2

WAKE ME UP WHEN SEPTEMBER ENDS — Green Day

AUGUST — Rilo Kiley

FOURTH OF JULY — Fall Out Boy

LAST JUNE — Gallows

MONTH OF MAY — Arcade Fire

APRIL SKIES — The Jesus and Mary Chain

DEATH MARCH — Motionless in White

FEBRUARY STARS — Foo Fighters

ROCK KNOWLEDGE

The Rolling Stones' iconic tongue logo was inspired not by Mick Jagger's kisser, but by the Indian Hindu goddess Kali The Destroyer, the ferocious form of the mother goddess.

ROCK'S MOST INVENTIVE ALBUM PROMO

John Freese is the drummer to the stars, the trusted tub-thumper for Nine Inch Nails, A Perfect Circle, Guns N' Roses, Weezer and many others. In 2009, however, Freese released Since 1972, his second solo release, and offered fans the chance to buy it in a number of tiered, value-added packages.

The levels ran from the basic $7 right up to a $75,000 premium. As the price increased with each package, so did the add-ons. Highlights at various tiers included: a five-minute "thank you" call from Josh for buying the album; the promise that he would wash your car or do your laundry; the chance to "get drunk and cut each other's hair in the parking lot of the Long Beach courthouse (filmed and posted on YouTube, of course)"; and a day at Disneyland. But for the prime package, you'd need to stump up $75,000, which would get you:

SINCE 1972

The $75,000 Package (limited edition of one)

Signed CD/DVD and digital download

✚ T-shirt

✚ Go on tour with Josh for a few days

✚ Have Josh write, record, and release a five-song EP about you and your life story

✚ Take home any of his drum sets (only one, but you can choose which one)

✚ Take 'shrooms and cruise Hollywood in Danny from Tool's Lamborghini
OR play quarters and then hop on the Ouija board for a while

✚ Josh will join your band for a month: play shows,
record, party with groupies, etc.

✚ If you don't have a band he'll be your personal assistant for
a month (4-day work weeks, 10am to 4pm)

✚ Take a limo down to Tijuana and he'll show you how it's done
(what that means exactly we can't legally get into here)

✚ If you don't live in southern California (but are a US resident) he'll come
to you and be your personal assistant/cabana boy for two weeks

✚ Take a flying trapeze lesson with Josh and Robin from NIN, go back to
Robin's place afterwards and his wife will make you raw lasagna

YOU'RE SO VAIN

Famous songs famous artists wrote about famous people.

ARTIST	★	SONG	★	INSPIRATION
Aerosmith	★	*Dude Looks Like a Lady*	★	Motley Crue's Vince Neil
Babyshambles	★	*Katy*	★	Kate Moss
The Beatles	★	*Hey Jude*	★	Julian Lennon
David Bowie	★	*Jean Genie*	★	Iggy Pop
Coldplay	★	*Fix You*	★	Gwyneth Paltrow
Sheryl Crow	★	*My Favorite Mistake*	★	Eric Clapton
Bob Dylan	★	*Like a Rolling Stone*	★	Andy Warhol
Foo Fighters	★	*I'll Stick Around*	★	Courtney Love
Lennie Kravitz	★	*It Ain't Over 'Til It's Over*	★	(ex-wife) Lisa Bonet
John Lennon	★	*How Do You Sleep?*	★	Paul McCartney
Courtney Love	★	*But Julian, I'm a Little Older Than You*	★	Julian Casablancas
John Mayer	★	*Paper Doll*	★	Taylor Swift
John Mayer	★	*Your Body Is a Wonderland*	★	Jennifer Love Hewitt
Don Mclean	★	*American Pie*	★	Buddy Holly
Nirvana	★	*Heart Shaped Box*	★	Courtney Love
Oasis	★	*Cast No Shadow*	★	Richard Ashcroft (The Verve)
Oasis	★	*Live Forever*	★	Kurt Cobain*
Paul Simon	★	*Hearts and Bones*	★	Carrie "Princess Leia" Fisher
Gwen Stefani	★	*Hollaback Girl*	★	Courtney Love
Suede	★	*Daddy's Speeding*	★	James Dean
U2	★	*Stuck in a Moment You Can't Get Out Of*	★	Michael Hutchence
The Velvet Underground	★	*Femme Fatale*	★	Edie Sedgwick (actress)
Amy Winehouse	★	*Me and Mr Jones*	★	(Rapper) Nas

*Inspired by Cobain's suicidal tendencies, rather than by the Nirvana frontman

ROCK ★ KNOWLEDGE

To break the ice at parties, Kurt Cobain would enter the room with the words "Here we are now: entertain us." Parties were awkward to Cobain. "It's really boring and uncomfortable," he said, "so it was, 'Well, here we are; entertain us'."

The term colitas – as in "warm smell of colitas" – in The Eagles' *Hotel California* means "little tails" in Spanish. Which makes no sense. The fact that in Mexican slang colitas refers to the buds of the cannabis plant does, however, add up.

It is thought – though not categorically proven – that the term "rock and roll" was coined by Maurie Orodenker, a columnist on US Billboard magazine. Orodenker used the phrase in 1942, to refer to more upbeat recordings.

Those screams you can hear when the green fairy (Kylie Minogue) turns evil in the film Moulin Rouge? Provided by the Prince of Darkness himself, Ozzy Osbourne. And the blood-curdling screams of the undead dead in *I Am Legend*? They came courtesy of Faith No More frontman Mike Patton.

Sex Pistol John Lydon was meant to be on the Lockerbie flight that was blown up by a terrorist bomb in 1988. He only missed it because his wife hadn't packed her case in time.

ANATOMY OF... A TURNTABLE

Put the needle to the record.

PLINTH

The base of the record player.

PLATTER/BEARING

The part of the turntable that rotates, on which sits a soft, cushioning, vibration-reducing mat, onto which you place your vinyl.

SPEED SELECTOR

Switch between 33rpm for long players and 12-inchers, 45rpm for 7-inch, 78rpm for old-timers.

START/STOP

This button turns on the motor, which spins the platter/bearing.

CUING LEVER

With this you raise or lower the stylus, off or onto the record. This is where you, as the saying goes, cue the music. It can be automatic or manual.

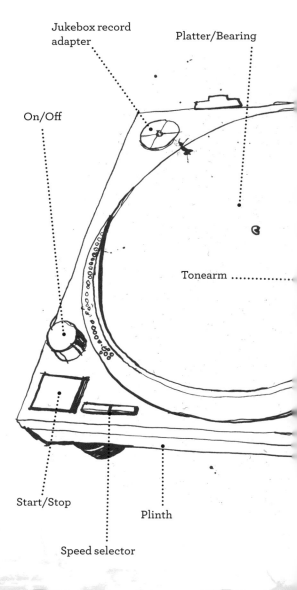

Jukebox record adapter

Platter/Bearing

On/Off

Tonearm

Start/Stop

Plinth

Speed selector

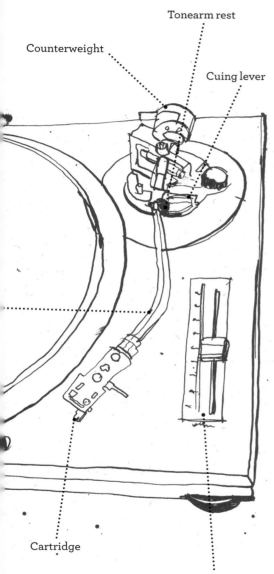

Counterweight

Tonearm rest

Cuing lever

Cartridge

Pitch control

TONEARM

Holds the headshell, which holds the cartridge, which holds the stylus. The cartridge converts the movement of the stylus into an electrical signal and creates sweet music. Over time and through repeated use, the stylus will need replacing.

TONEARM REST

This allows you to rest the tonearm safely when not in use.

COUNTERWEIGHT

An adjustable weight that allows you to fine-tune how much force the needle applies to the surface of the record. Tinker here with caution.

CARTRIDGE

This holds the stylus (the needle) and converts the movement of the stylus into an electrical signal, which becomes glorious sound.

PITCH CONTROL

Aka a Pitch Adjustment or Pitch Fader, this sliding switch allows you to adjust the rotation speed of the platter. Essential for DJs.

"YEAH, JUST TAKE A LEFT AT **FLAMING LIPS ALLEY**"

You know you've made it when they name a street, straat, or Strasse in your honour.

AC/DC LANE
– Melbourne, Australia

ANTHRAX STREET
– Fayetteville, North Carolina

BOB DYLAN WAY
– Duluth, Minnesota

DAVE GROHL ALLEY
– Warren, Ohio

ELVIS PRESLEY BOULEVARD
– Memphis, Tennessee

FLAMING LIPS ALLEY
– Oklahoma City, Oklahoma

FRANK ZAPPA STRASSE
– Berlin, Germany

GEORGE HARRISON WAY
– Liverpool, England

JIMI HENDRIX WAY
– Bellingham, Washington

JIMI HENDRIXSTRAAT
– Almere, Netherlands

JOEY RAMONE PLACE
– Manhattan, New York City

JOHN LENNON DRIVE
– Liverpool, England

KORN ROW
– Bakersfield, California

PAUL MCCARTNEY WAY
– Liverpool, England

RINGO STARR DRIVE
– Liverpool, England

ROLLING STONESSTRAAT
– Almere, Netherlands

TOM PETTY ROAD
– Dickson, Tennessee

U2 WAY
– Manhattan, New York City
(temporarily named)

THEY FOUGHT THE LAW / THE LAW WON

JOHNNY CASH

Apprehended while either picking flowers on private property or simply for walking to buy cigarettes long after the Starkville, Mississippi, city curfew on 11 May 1965, all that can be said for certain was that the Man in Black was intoxicated. Tossed in the can to sober up, he broke one of his big toes attempting to kick down the door. By the time he was set free, he had a new song – Starkville City Jail – and his 15-year-old cellmate had a new pair of shoes. "Here's a souvenir," he announced as he handed them over. "I'm Johnny Cash."

26 BANDS THAT CHANGED THEIR NAMES

SOME CHANGED FOR LEGAL REASONS, OTHERS JUST HAD A CHANGE OF HEART.

WHO?	BECAME	THEM!
Can of Piss		R.E.M.
Free Beer		Barenaked Ladies
Death From Above		Death From Above 1979
Gamma Ray		Queens of the Stone Age
The High Numbers		The Who
Hybrid Theory		Linkin Park
The Hype		U2
Jimmy James & The Blue Flames		Jimi Hendrix Experience
Mighty Joe Young		Stone Temple Pilots
Mookie Blaylock		Pearl Jam
Mr. Crowe's Garden		The Black Crowes
The New Yardbirds		Led Zeppelin
The Obelisk		The Cure
On a Friday		Radiohead
The Other Gang		Black Rebel Motorcyle Club
Polka Tulk Blues Band		Black Sabbath
Rat Salad became		Van Halen
The Screaming Abdabs		Pink Floyd
Seymour became		Blur
The Sex Maggots		Goo Goo Dolls
The Silver Beatles		The Beatles
Smile		Queen
Sweet Children		Green Day
Tony Flow and the Miraculously Majestic Masters of Mayhem		Red Hot Chili Peppers
Ted, Ed, Fred		Nirvana
The Weak Heartdrops		The Clash

NEW YORK!
NEW YORK!

No city in the world has been serenaded in song more often than the Big Apple. So why not take a brief, selective tour with some of the city's best tracks?

8 Manhattan

19 The whole city

1.
Avenue B by Iggy Pop (1999)
On New York's Lower East Side, where Iggy used to live and score his naughty drugs.

2.
Coney Island by Death Cab for Cutie (2001)
A near neighbour of The Velvet Underground's Coney Island Baby.

3.
Desolation Row by Bob Dylan (1965)
Supposedly a stretch of Eighth Avenue that was beyond renovation or redemption.

4.
Incident on 57th Street by Bruce Springsteen (1973)
The tale of Spanish Johnny, with his bruised arms, broken rhythm, and a beat-up old Buick.

5.
Empire State by Fleetwood Mac (1982)
Full of tourists but affords magnificent views. Possibly drug related.

6.
Fifth Avenue New York City by The Vandals (1967)
Excellent retail options round here.

7.

I'm Waiting for the Man by **The Velvet Underground** (1967)

Loitering on the intersection of Lexington Avenue and 125th Street, to buy heroin. As you do.

8.

Manhattan by **Cat Power** (2012)

A Kings of Leon track of the same name is actually about the plight of the Native Americans, not about the Big Apple.

9.

Positively 4th Street by **Bob Dylan** (1965)

Many theories suggest this refers to the Greenwich Village street on which Dylan once lived.

10.

Skylines and Turnstiles by **My Chemical Romance** (2002)

Written about the September 11, 2001, terror attack on the city.

11.

M79 by **Vampire Weekend** (2008)

Named after a Manhattan bus route.

12.

10th Avenue Freeze-Out by **Bruce Springsteen** (1975)

Likely to be the avenue running up the lower half of Manhattan, though Springsteen himself says he doesn't know the story behind the song, or at least he isn't telling.

13.

Angel of Harlem by **U2** (1988)

A homage to Billie Holiday, who spent her formative years in the north Manhattan neighbourhood.

14.

Brooklyn Bound by **The Black Keys** (2002)

Once an alternative for those pushed out of pricey Manhattan. Now, not so much.

15.

Chelsea Hotel Nights by **Ryan Adams** (2004)

Where Sid Vicious allegedly killed his girlfriend.

16.

Daughters of the SoHo Riots by **The National** (2005)

Not in the wrong city, but South of Houston Street.

17.

Ludlow Street by **Julian Casablancas** (2009)

Home to a number of live music venues, not to mention the legendary Katz's Delicatessen.

18.

Off Broadway by **Ryan Adams** (2007)

More tourists unfortunately

19.

Yeah! New York by **Yeah Yeah Yeahs** (2003)

The whole apple

SCHOOL OF ROCK

How to… Behave at a Gig

Rules for the modern gig-goer.

LEAVE YOUR CAMERA IN YOUR POCKET

If you absolutely have to take an out-of-focus shot of small people standing on stage and obscured by a load of heads, make it quick and keep it to an absolute minimum. Keep your phone's screen brightness down on a low setting, turn the f***ing flash off, and don't spend more than four seconds uploading the results to any social network.

NEVER THROW YOUR DRINK IN THE AIR WHEN THE BAND KICKS OFF

It might seem like a good idea in your head – the very essence of the rock 'n' roll spirit even – but it never can, and never does, end well.

KEEP YOUR NOISE DOWN

Standing in silence throughout a gig would be weird, but remember that your fellow gig-goers have come to listen to the band, not to you rambling on at high volume about cheese or taxis. And particularly not during the quiet, intimate, acoustic bits. If you have to talk, talk quietly.

TRY REALLY HARD NOT TO BE SICK ON ANYONE

A hot, sweaty atmosphere, combined with those wild, jerky, pogo-ey exertions we call dancing can often result in a queasy, uncertain feeling that builds from the pit of your stomach and soon presents itself in a Technicolor puddle at your feet. If you feel an imminent gush, bolt for the bogs.

NO STAGE-DIVING

It's obviously risky, but it happens. Don't dream of doing it if it's not permitted by the venue, the band, or (crucially) the band's very muscular security guys. If it's not permitted, those muscular men will manhandle you from the stage, through the doors, and head first into the street, and you'll have no one to blame but yourself.

MOSH NICE

If one of those snarly mosh pits opens up and you feel the urge to bump and bang about with a bunch of sweaty strangers, respect that not everybody will feel so inclined. Never attempt to pull others in, unless they clearly want to get involved.

PARENTAL ADVISORY EXPLICIT LYRICS

THE FILTHY 15

★★★★★★★★★★★★★★★★★★

In 1985, America's Parents Music Resource Center (PMRC) composed a playlist of songs deemed the most offensive of the time. Dubbed the "Filthy 15", the list was created to illustrate how albums should be rated, based on their content: X for profanity or sexually explicit lyrics; D/A for references to drugs and/or alcohol; O for occult references; and V for violent content. In the end, America opted for "Parental Advisory: Explicit Lyrics" stickers instead. But these were the original Filthy 15.

ROCK KNOWLEDGE

Frank Zappa's 1986 album Jazz from Hell was released with an "Explicit lyrics" warning sticker on the cover, even though the album is entirely instrumental.

BAND	TRACK	OFFENCE
AC/DC	*Let Me Put My Love into You*	**Sex**
Black Sabbath	*Trashed*	**Drug and alcohol use**
Sheena Easton	*Sugar Walls*	**Sex**
Cyndi Lauper	*She-Bop*	**Sex**
Def Leppard	*High 'n Dry*	**Drug and alcohol use**
Judas Priest	*Eat Me Alive*	**Sex**
Madonna	*Dress You Up*	**Sex**
Mary Jane Girls	*In My House*	**Sex**
Mercyful Fate	*Into the Coven*	**Occult**
Mötley Crüe	*Bastard*	**Violence**
Prince	*Darling Nikki*	**Sex**
Twisted Sister	*We're Not Gonna Take It*	**Violence**
Vanity	*Strap On "Robbie Baby"*	**Sex**
W.A.S.P.	*Animal (F*ck Like a Beast)*	**Sex**
Venom	*Possessed*	**Occult**

STATUES OF LIBERTY!

Eight large statues that honour rock legends.

JIMI HENDRIX

What: Life-size bronze of Hendrix in classic on-knees, Strat-wailing pose.
Where: Capitol Hill, Seattle, Washington.

BON SCOTT
(AC/DC)

What: Life-size, lung-busting bronze statue of Scott, stood on an amp.
Where: Fishing Boat Harbour, in his home town of Fremantle, Australia.

JERRY GARCIA
(Grateful Dead)

What: Immortalized as a strange tree-man-type creation, entitled "Bronze Garcia".
Where: Edgefield, near Portland, Oregon.

JOHNNY RAMONE
(The Ramones)

What: Eight-foot (2.4-m) bronze statue of the legendary Ramone, playing his guitar.
Where: Hollywood Forever Cemetery, Los Angeles.

FREDDIE MERCURY
(Queen)

What: Ten-foot (3-m) tall Freddie, set in concert pose, with clenched fist raised to the heavens.
Where: Montreux, Switzerland.

JOHN LENNON
(The Beatles)

What: Life-size bronze statue of the Beatle, sat cross-legged on a park bench.
Where: John Lennon Parque, Havana, Cuba.

KURT COBAIN
(Nirvana)

What: Concrete "crying" statue, featuring a single, sad, solitary tear rolling down his cheek.
Where: Cobain's home town, at the Aberdeen Museum of History, Aberdeen, Washington.

LEMMY
(Motörhead)

What: A life-size, $20,000 statue of the legendary Motörhead frontman, currently in production.
Where: The front of Lemmy's beloved Rainbow Bar & Grill in Hollywood, California, soon.

* *

In this series, we have chosen some of our favourite performers; the artists who embody the Marshall spirit. These are some of the true pioneers of rock – the Legends of Loud.

PJ HARVEY
The Dark Dame of Dorset

Of all the many singer-songwriting female artists thrown into the spotlight by the early Nineties alt-rock explosion, few have stood the test of time as well as Polly Jean Harvey. Growing up on a sheep farm in Yeovil, Somerset, England, the daughter of a quarryman father and an artist mother, Harvey was raised on a diet of vinyl: Howlin' Wolf, Bob Dylan, The Rolling Stones, John Lee Hooker, and Nina Simone shaped her formative years. "My mother and father are very involved with music," she recalled. "It's completely part of their soul."

She grew up an artist in the truest sense of the word, turning down a place to study sculpture at London's University for the Arts at Central Saint Martin's to pursue her true calling. Via a stint in Automatic Dlamini, she formed a three-piece in her own name, PJ Harvey, and unleashed debut album *Dry*. A dark, primal slice of feminine aggression that explored the themes of sex, love, and religion with an honest brutality, the album shook the world

and saw *Rolling Stone* magazine name her "Best Songwriter" and "Best New Female Singer" in 1992. The follow-up album, *Rid of Me* only confirmed their faith.

Over the following two decades, further albums have brought numerous accolades, most notably two Mercury Prizes (in 2001 and 2011, the only artist to receive the award twice), and an MBE for services to music in 2013.

Unlike all too many artists, PJ Harvey appears to be getting better with time, age, and experience. "Making me into a role model is placing too much importance on what I see as a work in progress," she says. In other words, her best is yet to come.

ROCK'S SIX GREATEST GUITAR GODS

Despite there being waaaaaaay too many to choose from, the following six men
all deserve special mention. Let the arguments begin!

1.
JIMI HENDRIX

The greatest axe-wielder the world has ever witnessed died almost 50 years ago, but his influence will seep through rock music forever more. Hendrix redefined what rock music could be, his manipulation of the Stratocaster creating sounds that came from another planet and another dimension. It was primal, pioneering, and effortless, but only for him.

His finest hour... *All Along the Watchtower*

2.
MATT BELLAMY (MUSE)

An elder guitar snob might raise an eyebrow at the presence of Matt Bellamy on this list, yet he is the most prolific axeman at work today. Bellamy's penchant for searing solos and raging, rampaging riffs is the single reason Muse have graduated from toilet tours to the full-blown stadium rock gods they are today.

His finest hour... *Plug in Baby*

3.
JACK WHITE (THE WHITE STRIPES)

Though so often sidetracked on production duty and by lending his vocals to other projects, Jack White's day job involves waging war on his guitar. "I always look at playing guitar as an attack," he says. "It has to be a fight: every song, every guitar solo, every note." Based on the evidence, it's a fight he's clearly winning.

His finest hour... *Ball and Biscuit*

4.
JOHN FRUSCIANTE (RED HOT CHILI PEPPERS)

With a fit and firing Frusciante on axe duty, the Chili Peppers unleashed Blood Sugar Sex Magic on the world, the blueprint of their sock-on-cock-rocking Californian funk. Without him, they released One Hot Minute. In short, the highs are far higher when he's involved.

His finest hour... *Turn It Again*

5.
TOM MORELLO (RAGE AGAINST THE MACHINE)

Placing greater emphasis on his effects pedals than any other man on this list, Morello redefined the role of the modern-day lead guitarist – he's part seismic shredder, part hip-hop DJ. The two roles combined to spectacular effect.

His finest hour... *Sleep Now in the Fire*

6.
PRINCE

Only making occasional forays into what we know as rock music, Prince graces this list for his cameo on the show-ending rendition of *While My Guitar Gently* Weeps at the 2004 Rock and Roll Hall of Fame ceremony. Search for the track, sit tight until 03:25, then bow down. That's why the mini maestro is here.

His finest hour... The above, plus *Purple Rain*

ALE HOUSE ROCK

The biggest names in rock brew their own booze, presumably just because they can.
However, not all ale is brewed equal…

THE BREWER	★	THE ALE	★	ABV
Elbow	★	Build a Rocket Boys!	★	4% ABV
Kid Rock	★	Badass	★	4.2% ABV
Status Quo	★	Piledriver	★	4.3% ABV
Iron Maiden	★	Trooper	★	4.7% ABV
Motörhead	★	Bastards	★	4.7% ABV
Queen	★	Bohemian Lager	★	4.7% ABV
Frank Turner	★	Believe	★	4.8% ABV
Reverend & the Makers	★	American Brown	★	5% ABV
Maximo Park	★	Maximo No.5	★	5% ABV
Enter Shikari	★	Sssnakepit	★	5% ABV
Pearl Jam	★	Faithfull Ale	★	7% ABV
Hanson *	★	MmmHops	★	7.5% ABV
Mastodon	★	Black Tongue	★	8.3% ABV
Super Furry Animals	★	Fuzzy	★	8.5% ABV
Marshall	★	Blonde Craft Beer	★	8.6% ABV

*(yes, we know they're not rock, but what a name and just look at that ABV)

THEY FOUGHT THE LAW / THE LAW WON
LIAM GALLAGHER

Manchester-born mouthpiece Liam Gallagher stumbled into trouble at Munich's Bayerischer Hof hotel during an Oasis tour in 2002, having flicked peanuts at the wrong set of revelers. Initially reported as being local gangsters, Gallagher's targets turned out to be just a group of real estate agents and computer salesmen enjoying a night out. But they took exception to having nuts flicked their way, and in the ensuing altercation, Gallagher had his two front teeth knocked out and was arrested for kicking a policeman. He escaped jail time after paying a very hefty fine.

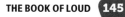

HOUSES OF THE HOLY

The most iconic rock venues in the world
– past and present.

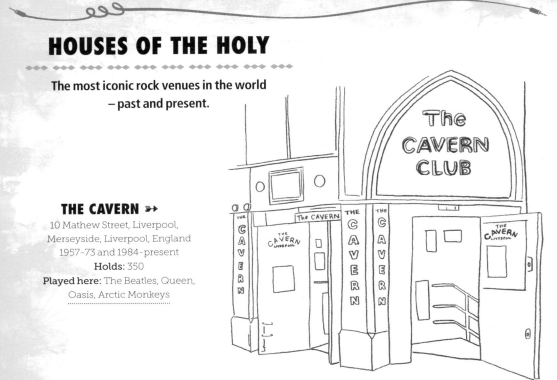

THE CAVERN ➤➤

10 Mathew Street, Liverpool,
Merseyside, Liverpool, England
1957-73 and 1984-present
Holds: 350
Played here: The Beatles, Queen,
Oasis, Arctic Monkeys

THE FILLMORE

1805 Geary Boulevard, San Francisco, California, USA
1912-71 and 1994-present
Holds: 1,100
Played here: The Grateful Dead, Jimi Hendrix,
Radiohead, The White Stripes

THE ROXY

9009 West Sunset Boulevard, West Hollywood,
California, USA
1973-present
Holds: 500
Played here: Neil Young, Sex Pistols,
Red Hot Chili Peppers, Kings of Leon

KING TUT'S WAH WAH HUT

272a St Vincent Street, Glasgow, Scotland
1990-present
Holds: 300
Played here: Oasis, The Killers,
Radiohead, My Chemical Romance

THE ASTORIA

157 Charing Cross Road, London, England
1985-2009
Held: 2,000
Played here: Radiohead, Smashing Pumpkins,
Metallica, Nirvana

WHISKY A GO GO

8901 W. Sunset Boulevard, West Hollywood,
California, USA
1964-present
Holds: 250
Played here: The Doors, Janis Joplin, Led Zeppelin

THE TROUBADOUR

9081 Santa Monica Boulevard, West Hollywood,
California, USA
1957-present
Holds: 400
Played here: The Doors, Guns N' Roses,
Radiohead, The White Stripes

MARQUEE CLUB

90 Wardour Street, Soho, London, England
1964-88
Held: 1,400
Played here: Jimi Hendrix, Pink Floyd,
The Cure, Joy Division, Metallica, the Sex Pistols

THE CROCODILE

2200 2nd Avenue, Seattle, Washington, USA
1991-2007 and 2009-present
Holds: 525
Played here: Nirvana, Pearl Jam,
Beastie Boys, Dinosaur Jr.

BRIXTON ACADEMY

211 Stockwell Road, Brixton, London, England
1981-present
Holds: 4,921
Played here: Faith No More, Arcade Fire,
Bob Dylan, Nine Inch Nails

◄◄ CBGB

315 Bowery, Manhattan,
New York, New York, USA
1973-2006
Held: 300-350
Played here: The Ramones,
Blondie, Talking Heads,
Patti Smith

THE VINYL DICTIONARY

****

A latecomer to buying vinyl? Allow this glossary to fill in the basic gaps.

BOOTLEG – An illegal pressing, usually recorded at a concert without the band or record company's permission. Just say no, kids.

CATALOGUE NUMBER – Almost every commercial release features one, usually a combination of numbers and letters and prefaced with "Cat no". Promo copies feature different numbers, often prefixed with "PRO" or "PR".

CUSTOM SLEEVE – A picture or stickered sleeve used for promotional pressings, making it more sought after than the commercial version.

COLORED VINYL – Available in any colour other than black, and often more sought-after as a result.

EP – Extended Play. Usually a 7-inch 45 record with two or three tracks per side.

FIRST PRESSING/ISSUE – First version of a record, adding to its scarcity value.

GATEFOLD – Common on LPs and EPs, the sleeve folds down the centre and then opens up like a gate. Often abbreviated as "g/fold" or "g/f".

JACKET – Outer sleeve, inside which lives the inner sleeve, inside which lives the record.

The two layers are designed to protect the delicate vinyl from scratches.

LIMITED EDITION – Rarer than regular issue releases, sending the demand and price up as a result. Often numbered and often abbreviated as 'Ltd Edn'.

LP – Even the novice knows: long play, a long-player, your music cut onto two sides of wax. Usually used for 10-inch and 12-inch 33⅓ albums.

LEAD-IN GROOVE – The silent area at the beginning of a record. The crackly calm before the storm.

MATRIX NUMBER – Numbers etched into the run-off groove. Acts as a barcode to identify the release.

OBI-STRIP – A narrow strip of paper wrapped around the sleeve of Japanese releases. Screams "Rare", except in Japan, where it screams "Normal".

POLYVINYL CHLORIDE – What you know as vinyl: the flexible material used since the 1930s to make the object of your desire.

REISSUE – As the title suggests, not the original issue. Often this can be a budget reissue and usually it will be of lesser value as a result.

RPM – Revolutions (of the record) per minute. Albums play at 33⅓ RPM, EPs and seven-inch records spin at 45 RPM.

SHAPED DISC – Vinyl disc cut into a quirky shape – a pineapple, for example, or a cat – with a regular 7-inch or 10-inch playing area included in the design. Usually a more limited release.

SLEEVE – Inner papery protection, into which you slide the record. The sleeve then lives inside the jacket.

TEST PRESSING – An early pressing of a work, often sent out as a promotional version before the full record was finished, and frequently without artwork. Often abbreviated as "T/P" and harder to come by.

WARPING – When exposed to heat, your vinyl bends and warps. This is not a good thing.

WHITE LABEL – A promo version featuring a white label with very limited band and track details.

ROCK AND RING!

Eleven of the most popular first dance wedding tunes.

You Are the Best Thing
by Ray LaMontagne

First Day of My Life
by Bright Eyes

Marry Me
by Train

Better Together
by Jack Johnson

Crazy Love
by Van Morrison

Iris
by Goo Goo Dolls

I Don't Want to Miss a Thing
by Aerosmith

Baby I'm Yours
by Arctic Monkeys

Fade into You
by Mazzy Star

I Will Follow You into the Dark
by Death Cab for Cutie

Forever
by Ben Harper

Source: Spotify, taken from 12,000 single-track playlists named 'First Dance'.

THE STYLE OF ROCK: *ROCK OUTFITS*

A visual celebration of some of rock music's most legendary outfits.

THE REBEL REBEL ⚑

As rocked by David Bowie. The Thin White Duke went all colour-blind pirate in 1974, rocking a look never bettered and very rarely attempted since. Adam and his Ants were clearly inspired, though, basing their entire look on this single classic cut.

THE SGT. PEPPER ⚑

As rocked by The Beatles. To record an album in the style of an Edwardian-era military band – in this case Sgt. Pepper's Lonely Hearts Club Band – The Beatles decided they must dress as an Edwardian-era military band.

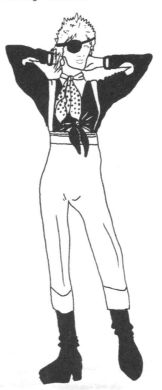

THE SCHOOLBOY ⚑

As rocked by AC/DC's Angus Young. Still worn to this day by the Aussie axe god, despite the fact Angus is now over 60. He claims it to be a "distinctively classic look".

THE RED OR DEAD ♥

As rocked by Marilyn Manson. For a man usually drenched in gothic shades of black, this red-top-hat-and-trench-coat look represented a daring and unexpected departure: the Willy Wonka of our nightmares.

THE HELMETS ⚑

As rocked by Daft Punk. Two magnificently buffed-up helmets hide the faces of enigmatic French electronic two-piece Guy-Manuel de Homem-Christo and Thomas Bangalter. Two sharp and shiny suits complete the look.

THE PEARLY KING ⚑

As rocked by The White Stripes. Created for the cover of Icky Thump, the his-and-hers, Cockney-inspired tuxedos worn by Jack and Meg White were painstakingly adorned with 13,000 hand-stitched buttons on each suit.

THE SPOTTER'S GUIDE :
THE METAL KID

Here, learn how to spot the embodiment of rock, the metal kid.

Entry-level piercings to nose, lip, and eyebrows. Face paint exhibited among fans of Kiss and GWAR.

Tattoo count will vary from a light smattering to a full body. Expect skulls, snakes, and Beelzebub himself.

Band T-shirt, available in any colour as long as it's black. Band name at owner's discretion, but usually AC/DC, GN'R, Led Zeppelin, or Maiden. Cut-off sleeves optional and allow for improved flailing once the gig begins.

Studded bracelet, studded belt, and, for the real showmen, studded codpiece.

Trousers are dirty denim or leather, worn slightly tighter than looks comfortable. (Note: fans of 1980s' hair-metal bands swap the denim or leather for spandex.)

Heavy-metal footwear ranges from big black boots to smaller black boots. The common theme here, of course, is the colour.

Hair worn long, despite the best efforts of nature and gravity. Grease entirely natural.

In colder climes, the metalhead will wear a jacket: always leather, always black, and usually adorned with band patches, assorted badges, and stale ale.

Listening to:

Led Zeppelin, *Led Zeppelin IV*

AC/DC, *Back in Black*

Iron Maiden, *The Number of the Beast*

Van Halen, *Van Halen*

Guns N' Roses, *Appetite for Destruction*

Metallica, *Metallica*

Queens of the Stone Age, *Songs for the Deaf*

Slipknot, *Slipknot*

Black Sabbath, *Paranoid*

Korn, *Korn*

System Of A Down, *Toxicity*

Black Sabbath, *Black Sabbath*

Metallica, *Master Of Puppets*

Tool, *Lateralus*

Motörhead, *Ace Of Spades*

NO, THANKS

Not all bands accept their place in the Rock and Roll Hall of Fame. Axl Rose refused his place in 2012, writing a very lengthy but oddly reasonable screed on why he wouldn't accept his place. And he was following in the footsteps of the Sex Pistols, who in 1996 posted a handwritten letter to their own website explaining why they wouldn't accept. It was as eloquent, poorly punctuated, and warm-hearted as expected and read:

"Next to the SEX PISTOLS, rock and roll and that hall of fame is a piss stain. Your museum. Urine in wine. Were not coming. Were not your monkey and so what? Fame at $25,000 if we paid for a table, or $15,000 to squeak up in the gallery, goes to a non-profit organisation selling us a load of old famous. Congradulations. If you voted for us, hope you noted your reasons. Your anonymous as judges, but your still music industry people. Were not coming. Your not paying attention. Outside the shit-stem is a real SEX PISTOL"

LONG-PLAYING LUNACY

27 unexpected (and ill-advised) album titles.

WHEN	★	ALBUM TITLE	★	BAND
1968	★	*Bang, Bang You're Terry Reid*	★	Terry Reid
1968	★	*My People Were Fair and Had Sky In Their Hair... But Now They're Content to Wear Stars on Their Brows*	★	T. Rex
1971	★	*A Vulture Is Not a Bird You Can Trust*	★	Ian A. Anderson
1973	★	*Attempted Mustache*	★	Loudon Wainwright III
1973	★	*Brain Salad Surgery*	★	Emerson, Lake and Palmer
1978	★	*You Can Tune a Piano But You Can't Tuna Fish*	★	REO Speedwagon
1979	★	*Sheik Yerbouti*	★	Frank Zappa
1980	★	*Shark Sandwich*	★	Spinal Tap
1981	★	*The Adventures of Kaptain Kopter & Commander Cassidy in Potato Land*	★	Spirit
1982	★	*Angst in My Pants*	★	Sparks
1984	★	*The Pros and Cons of Hitch Hiking*	★	Roger Waters
1985	★	*Now! That's What I Call a F*cking Racket Vol. 1*	★	Chaotic Discord
1987	★	*Locust Abortion Technician*	★	Butthole Surfers
1988	★	*Hairway to Steven*	★	Butthole Surfers
1988	★	*OU812*	★	Van Halen
1990	★	*The Earth, a Small Man, His Dog and a Chicken*	★	REO Speedwagon

WHEN	ALBUM TITLE	BAND
1990	★ *The Earth, a Small Man, His Dog and a Chicken*	★ REO Speedwagon
1993	★ *Hairy Banjo*	★ Boyfriend
1995	★ *Vivadixiesubmarinetransmissionplot*	★ Sparklehorse
2000	★ *Chocolate Starfish and the Hot Dog Flavored Water*	★ Limp Bizkit
2002	★ *The Day They Shot a Hole in the Jesus Egg: 1989-1991*	★ The Flaming Lips
2003	★ *Who Will Cut Our Hair When We're Gone?*	★ The Unicorns
2004	★ *Uh Huh Her*	★ PJ Harvey
2008	★ *Professor Satchafunkilus and the Musterion of Rock*	★ Joe Satriani
2008	★ *This Is It and I Am It and You Are It and So Is That and He Is It and She Is It and It Is It and That Is That*	★ Marnie Stern
2009	★ *West Ryder Pauper Lunatic Asylum*	★ Kasabian
2012	★ *Kisses on the Bottom*	★ Paul McCartney

★ ★

THEY FOUGHT THE LAW / THE LAW WON

AXL ROSE

Arrested multiple times as the teenage delinquent William Bailey, Guns N' Roses front man W. Axl Rose kicked things up a notch or two in 1992 by inciting a riot. Enraged by a fan taking photos at Riverport, Missouri's Hollywood Casino Ampitheatre – in an era before mobile phones – Rose dived into the crowd to confiscate the offending camera. In doing so, the combustible front man lashed out at several members of his own security squad and ticket-paying fans. Upon returning to the stage he duly stormed off, sparking a riot that soon saw him arrested. Luckily for Rose, the judge found him guilty of little more than being a rock star.

INDEX

PICTURE CREDITS